"Brian and Teresa are like Chip and Joanna Gaines meet *The West Wing*. They have lots of heartwarming, poignant, and sometimes maddening tales about how government really works from their time in the White House. Plus their recipes will make your mouth water. A great book to read anytime, especially while drinking one of their delicious cocktails."

—**Buck Sexton**, Co-Host of *The Clay Travis & Buck Sexton Show*

"All American power couple Brian and Teresa Morgenstern have produced an absolutely unique and hilarious view of Washington, D.C. Lucky for us, they're taking readers along for a delicious ride with exquisite cocktails and tasty recipes. Everyone needs this book, but especially if you want to survive a career in politics."

—**Katie Pavlich**, Fox News Contributor and Editor of TownHall.com

"The book gives us such a personal and unique look at Teresa and Brian's experiences working inside the Trump administration. It's a fun and interesting read, and I can't wait to try the recipes and cocktails."

—**John Bachman**, Host of *John Bachman Now* on Newsmax

Vignettes & Vino

Vignettes & Vino

DINNER TABLE STORIES
from the **TRUMP WHITE HOUSE** with
RECIPES & COCKTAIL PAIRINGS

BRIAN & TERESA
MORGENSTERN

Post Hill
PRESS

A POST HILL PRESS BOOK

Vignettes & Vino:
Dinner Table Stories from the Trump White House with Recipes & Cocktail Pairings
© 2022 by Brian & Teresa Morgenstern
All Rights Reserved

ISBN: 978-1-63758-498-9
ISBN (eBook): 978-1-63758-499-6

Cover design by Cody Corcoran
Cover photo by Will DeGraw, Clever Disarray Photography
Photos courtesy of the authors unless otherwise specified.

This is a work of nonfiction. All people, locations, events, and situation are portrayed to the best of the author's memory.

Post Hill Press
New York • Nashville
posthillpress.com

Published in the United States of America
1 2 3 4 5 6 7 8 9 10

Contents

Introduction

Ie were never supposed to meet each other. According to the news
media, Donald Trump wasn't supposed to get elected president.
Neither of us was supposed to get a job in his administration. Neither
of us was supposed to go out to a party on a random Tuesday night in
Washington, D.C. But we did. And we met. And we fell in love.

Then COVID-19 happened. The hottest economy in history ground
to a halt because of a global pandemic. We found ourselves basically living together far sooner in our relationship than we had planned, because
we didn't want to quarantine alone. That could have gone one of two
ways. Either the cracks in our relationship could have become fault lines
faster, or we could have grown closer together faster. Thank God it was
the latter.

When COVID-19 hit in early 2020, Brian was working at the Treasury Department, where he helped run relief programs designed to keep
Americans connected to their jobs and to provide them with liquidity.
This was a 24/7 effort. He remained involved in those efforts until July
2020, when he moved from the Treasury across the street to the White
House, to join the press and communications team for the home stretch
of the presidential election.

Teresa had been working at the Commerce Department handling
protocol, which means that her responsibilities heavily involved managing the Commerce Department secretary's travel schedule for foreign

trade missions and the like. When COVID arrived in early 2020, that stopped abruptly. There was no more travel, and everyone was told to work remotely. So, while Brian worked, Teresa cooked. And she cooked some absolutely amazing meals. That's where the recipe and cocktail pairings for this book came into play.

Then, in the summer of 2020, Teresa was asked to move over to the Pentagon to assume the role of deputy press secretary. From there, she was quickly detailed to the White House to work on Operation Warp Speed, as a Pentagon representative on the task force charged with creating vaccines five times faster than any other vaccine in history.

So there we were, working together at the highest levels of government during a pandemic, a presidential election, and riots across the country—oh, and an unexpected Supreme Court confirmation. Beyond what we learned by surviving a volatile media environment, viral outbreaks at the White House, and a rapidly changing society, perhaps the biggest lesson we learned is that at the end of the day, the things that truly matter the most are family, faith, and good food.

We hope you enjoy our stories, recipes, and cocktails with the people you love.

CHAPTER 1

Getting Stuck with Your Significant Other During the Pandemic

BY TERESA

At some point in many relationships, couples start to gravitate to longer stays at each other's respective homes. First-date drinks give way to dinners, and dinners can lead to late nights, and late nights can lead to weekend trips, and so on. After a while, if you're spending enough time together, it gets exhausting to do the constant back-and-forth to each other's places. Well, I had reached that point in my relationship with Brian. We were spending so much time together; we would trade off nights at each other's places. We also had reached the stage of knowing that we would get married one day, so this was a serious commitment at this point. (A word of advice: Learn from my past mistakes and wait until you find someone you know you'll marry before you move in together. Brian and I officially moved in together after we got engaged.)

This was the beginning of 2020. It was about the time that I started really noticing and thinking about COVID; the nightly news shows were starting to feature its spread in China as a segment. My job at the time was working for Secretary Wilbur Ross at the Department of Commerce, handling advance and protocol for the secretary's travels. And this was a very well-traveled principal and team that allowed me to travel all over the world.

During a trip to Guatemala in January 2020, we had a layover in Atlanta during the return leg. Hartsfield-Jackson is one of the world's busiest international airports. So of course there were signs everywhere at customs warning about the dangers, symptoms, and possible transmission of the coronavirus originating in Wuhan, China. At the time, only travelers from Wuhan were further screened at customs.

Fast-forward about a month, and my team at Commerce and I were planning our next major swing across the world—and this time, our focus was China. You see, the Department of Commerce is a place where several random priorities of the federal government go to live. The secretary has responsibility not only for many international trade issues, but also for the National Oceanic and Atmospheric Administration (NOAA), fisheries, semiconductors, foreign investments, and more. And at a time when relations with China were at an all-time high in terms of tension, Secretary Ross played an important diplomatic role. Tensions are still high today, and having a secretary with decades of business experience, and immeasurable wealth to show for it, is very helpful in cases like that.

The secretary had been to China on an official visit once before, and some of my teammates knew how to handle the visa process and, subsequently, how the embassy would behave in granting our visas. The visa application for China is long and interrogative. Giving the Chinese government every last detail about your life is unnerving. But as a representative of the U.S. government, I felt that in the end, I would be okay.

My team got together with our chief of staff, Mike Walsh, to discuss the ever-changing plans for our trip. The around-the-world swing would take us from London to Austria (or Geneva), then to Singapore for an international air show, and then to Shanghai and Beijing in China for high-level meetings. There was also talk of tacking on a stop in South Korea at the very end. I got excited for that one, since I'm half Korean and was born there.

A trip like this would be an undertaking like no other, given the small number of staff members we had to plan and advance travel around the world. Most of us would have to take ownership of planning two country stops each, and would have to grab volunteers from other offices to help us out. We were frantically filling out passport and visa applications for everyone who might have to go on the trip, just to cover our bases.

As we mapped out our logistics with our chief, he finally addressed the elephant in the room. "What is going on in China with COVID? We can't take an eighty-two-year-old man there and risk the secretary getting sick." Secretary Ross was indeed eighty-two, and was more well-traveled than any of us. He truly outtraveled us on every trip. We were always in awe of how he could keep up. (Maybe flying business class does the trick.)

My colleague who was the secretary's scheduler chimed in, "I'll get in touch with White House medical to see what they recommend." That was a smart move. But we all knew what the answer would be. It was a week before the Lunar New Year in China, and millions of people usually traveled across the country to celebrate the ancient tradition. China had been calling for that to be postponed, and Wuhan was already on lockdown. There was no way we were going to China, or anywhere in Asia for that matter. And I was okay with that.

It wasn't too long after that fateful meeting that I took my last trip with Commerce. We ended up cutting that heavy trip by more than half. I took on the London leg solo—it's one of my favorite cities—and spent ten days there, orchestrating several meetings with political and business leaders for the secretary.

Then a few days later, Brian and I took our last international trip for 2020. We headed to Paris for a long weekend getaway.

Soon after, we were told to start wearing masks in airports.

Then, in March 2020, we would be locked down entirely, starting with "fifteen days to slow the spread." Fifteen days. Suuuure.

Now, most men are crippled without women or a significant other when it comes to taking care of themselves. I know that this stereotype applies to Brian. When it became evident that we would have to hunker down together as a nation for fifteen days, or however long it would be, I immediately called him and told him he would have to hunker down with me. Otherwise, knowing Brian, if he were to stay by himself, he would microwave a Lean Cuisine meal every night and skip breakfast and lunch. Naturally, women are inclined to ensure that everyone is well-fed and happy.

Brian packed his bags and prepared to spend two weeks with me. It wasn't the first time we had spent several nights together before, but previous times had been on vacations. This would be a short-term move-in. So, with my cat and my boyfriend, I prepared to spend the next few weeks facing an unimaginable time in our nation and world. Logically, our first instinct was the same as everyone else's: go to Costco.

If you're wondering what the experience was like at one of the busiest Costcos in the nation, it was pure insanity. There was no toilet paper left. All the chicken was gone. The place had turned into a madhouse. We weren't wearing masks, because we'd been told they weren't useful. But we were wearing disposable gloves—thanks to my mother who was in the medical field. We ventured in to grab all the things we would need for endless cooking—and drinking. Most of that first quarantine Costco bill was attributable to wine.

I remember that Costco trip vividly, and I learned a lot from it. Many of the recipes in this book were born from it. Little did I know at the time that this "two-week" quarantine would lead to one of the greatest economic, social, and political impacts in our history.

My job was at a standstill, but Brian was still working at the Treasury Department in full force. He was part of the team that was responsible for creating some of the largest economic relief programs in history in just days. He and a small group of others worked tirelessly to create the Payment Protection Program (PPP). They worked day and night, receiving hundreds of calls and emails at all hours.

Meanwhile, my team couldn't do much in terms of going back into work physically or working over email. My job was all about travel, and that was completely halted. Thankfully, my team was composed of great people whom I call some of my closest friends to this day. We filled our time with Zoom meetings, and Zoom happy hours, and group texting about travel memories—and how we had truly dodged a bullet with that potential China trip.

In my spare time, I did what any dedicated, loving girlfriend would do: cook!

And that's where this book comes in. I, like millions of people around the world, elevated my cooking skills during quarantine. There is something truly therapeutic and rewarding about preparing food and cooking it for your loved ones and friends. The sense of accomplishment from completing a dish—and then being able to eat it!—is so satisfying. Now we are happy to share with you all of these dishes that we have put our personal twists on. And what's the perfect complement to our once-in-a-lifetime experiences and the dishes we made at that time? Drinks, of course! Enjoy!

Spicy Chicken Parm, BY TERESA

This recipe simplifies the process for making classic Chicken Parmesan. I've used basic ingredients to create a delicious, no-fail sauce with a little kick to it. This dish was a hit with Brian and my dad, who is a self-proclaimed aficionado of all things Italian.

SERVES 4

¼ cup extra-virgin olive oil, divided
1 medium yellow onion, diced
3 cloves garlic, minced
2 bay leaves
2 28-oz. cans whole, peeled San Marzano tomatoes
¼ cup fresh basil, divided
1 Tbsp. dried Italian-blend seasoning (like Morton & Bassett's)
½ tsp. sugar
Salt, pepper, and red pepper flakes to taste
½ cup all-purpose flour
2 eggs, beaten
1 cup panko breadcrumbs
½ cup finely chopped flat-leaf parsley
3 tsp. garlic powder, divided
1 cup freshly grated Parmesan cheese, plus extra for sprinkling on top
4 skinless, boneless chicken breasts, pounded thinly
1 8-oz. ball of mozzarella, sliced
Pasta of your choice (preferably linguine), cooked

Preheat the oven to 350°F. In a pan over medium-low heat, pour a layer of olive oil. Add in the diced onions, minced garlic, and bay leaves until fragrant. Carefully pour the canned tomatoes over the mixture. After simmering for 5 minutes, throw in some hand-torn basil (but save some for garnish later). While the tomatoes cook, add in the dried Italian-seasoning blend and 2 tsp. garlic powder. While stirring the sauce, be sure to crush the whole tomatoes as they get softer. Add in the sugar as well as the salt, pepper, and red pepper flakes to taste. Let the sauce continue to simmer on low heat for 15 minutes.

Meanwhile, prepare 3 shallow dishes for breading the chicken. Put the flour in one dish and season with salt and pepper. In the second dish, pour in the beaten eggs (add a splash of water). In the third dish, combine the panko crumbs, chopped parsley, 1 tsp. garlic powder, and grated Parmesan.

In a separate oven-safe pan, pour in 3 Tbsp. olive oil. Do not start to heat the oil yet, as it can heat fast while you're preparing the chicken. To prepare the chicken, take one chicken breast and dredge in the flour. After the flour, dip the chicken breast in the egg mixture. Then, dredge both sides of the chicken breast in the panko breadcrumbs mixture. Set the pan with the oil over medium-high heat. Once the oil is hot (you can test with a drop of flour—if it sizzles, it's ready), fry each chicken breast for about 4 minutes on each side until golden brown and crusty.

While the chicken breasts are frying, blend the finished tomato sauce using either a stand blender or an immersion blender. When the chicken is done, pour the sauce over each piece in the same pan. Then place slices of mozzarella on top. Grate fresh Parmesan over the mozzarella. Add more hand-torn basil to finish it off.

Bake the pan in the oven for 15 minutes. Then broil it for 2 minutes. Carefully remove the pan from the oven.

Serve over pasta with extra sauce, and garnish with more freshly grated Parmesan and basil.

TO DRINK

Chianti and Sambuca, BY BRIAN

As hard as we tried, we could not come up with a better pairing for chicken Parmesan than a full, flavorful glass of Chianti, a classic Italian red wine. Torraiolo makes an excellent, modestly priced vintage.

After dinner, chilled sambuca makes for a delicious digestif, and we'd go with Romana white sambuca. We learned years ago at an Italian restaurant that the proper way to drink sambuca is chilled, with three coffee beans floating in it to represent health, happiness, and prosperity.

Pour the sambuca in a shaker with ice, shake well, and strain into a short glass. Drop three coffee beans on top and watch them float. Then toast to *la bella vita.*

CHAPTER 2

Executive Producer Steven T. Mnuchin

BY BRIAN

On Tax Day, April 17, 2018, CNBC's morning show *Squawk Box* broadcast live from the Rayburn Reception Room of the U.S. Capitol. I was there to staff Treasury Secretary Steven Mnuchin for his interview. It was a dream morning for every pro-growth, supply-side economics nerd in America. Appearances on the show would include Mnuchin, Office of Management and Budget (OMB) director (and future chief of staff) Mick Mulvaney, Ways and Means chairman Kevin Brady, CEO of the Business Roundtable and former White House chief of staff and former OMB director Josh Bolten. And the list goes on. They were all celebrating the first Tax Day after the passage of the Tax Cuts and Jobs Act (or, as President Trump wanted to call it, "Cut Cut Cut"), a signature achievement of the Trump administration. It was a real hoot.

I was in the green room (a conference room near the Rayburn Room) when Director Mulvaney and former Director Bolten practically ran right into each other. They are both Caucasian gentlemen of modest stature (much like myself) who wear glasses (sometimes like myself). Bolten entered the room just as Mulvaney turned around towards the door to leave. They were so close that they nearly clunked foreheads together. They each looked the other in the eye, and Mulvaney said, "Mr. Director." Then Bolten said, "Mr. Director."

It reminded me of the scene in the movie *Spies Like Us* where Chevy Chase and Dan Aykroyd walk into a military tent full of about ten doctors, who keep introducing themselves and calling each other "doctor." No one says anything but the word "doctor" over and over again for a full minute.

After a few pleasantries, everyone who had completed their TV interview left, and I waited for Secretary Mnuchin to arrive for his interview. He came in a few minutes ahead of time and made a beeline for the food spread. He filled his plate with some eggs and bacon, and fixed a cup of coffee. Then he sat down at the table to enjoy his breakfast.

I sat down a couple of seats away and put a document full of headlines and talking points in front of him, so that he would have something to review before going on camera. The secretary looked it over, picked it up, and flipped it back to me. This was pretty typical. I was his chief speechwriter at the time, and whenever I brought him drafts of remarks or memos, he would look them over and flip them back to me. If he liked what I'd given him, he would say that my work was "brilliant." Other times, he would point at the paper as if he wanted me to start writing something down, and then essentially dictate what he wanted to say. And on a couple of rare occasions, he would say something like, "Don't take this the wrong way, but I don't like it." (How could I take that the wrong way? It's so subtle!)

In any event, I genuinely appreciated Secretary Mnuchin's concise and straightforward way of doing business and approaching speaking engagements. It's reminiscent of the famous Winston Churchill quote, which is probably inappropriate by today's standards but gets the point across: "A good speech should be like a woman's skirt; long enough to cover the subject and short enough to create interest."

On this occasion, we had a few extra minutes before the secretary's TV hit, so we discussed what TV shows or movies we had seen recently.

The thing about discussing TV or movies with Steven Mnuchin is that it is very intimidating. Before becoming Treasury Secretary, he had been on the board of Goldman Sachs, bought a bank out of bankruptcy and brought it back to life, and founded a movie investment firm, which led to his being an executive producer of countless blockbuster hits. Some of his box office smashes include *American Sniper*, *Suicide Squad*, *Wonder Woman*, and *The Lego Batman Movie*. In fact, he once received an ethics complaint from some joyless liberal for jokingly "endorsing" Lego Batman in response to a friendly question at a public event; the person claimed that he was using his official position to promote his movie.

During our movie discussion, Mnuchin spoke about his guiding philosophy for successful films. He said, "People like three kinds of movies: rags to riches, riches to rags, and redemption." I suppose that's true to a degree. Virtually any good movie could meet at least one of those three descriptions.

After our discussion, the secretary went into the Rayburn Room and did his interview on CNBC. Towards the end of the interview, he and cohost Joe Kernen had an exchange about how they were enjoying the special site that day—the U.S. Capitol.

You see, Mnuchin had been considering the possibility of having *Squawk Box* broadcast live from the Treasury Department for months. The Cash Room at the U.S. Treasury Department is an incredible space. It has marble with gold leaf and soaring ceilings, and the secretary wanted to show it off to the American people. The Cash Room once served as the "bankers' bank" and had a vault full of gold bars, bank notes, and cash. It played host to the inaugural ball for President Ulysses S. Grant and countless other historic events. During our administration, we hosted a dinner with President Trump and the Emir of Qatar in the Cash Room.

Secretary Mnuchin told Kernen on air that Tony (referring to Assistant Secretary Tony Sayegh) would set it up so we could do a broadcast from the Cash Room. The hosts of *Squawk Box* were ecstatic and said they couldn't wait to do it.

However, we had not considered the need to treat other business networks fairly and to "spread the wealth" in terms of access to senior officials. And so we changed course.

A few months later, we hosted *Mornings with Maria* for the Fox Business Network with Maria Bartiromo in the Cash Room. It was epic. Every major player from the administration was there: Lynda McMahon from the Small Business Administration (former CEO of World Wrestling Entertainment, or WWE); the great Larry Kudlow, the president's economic advisor; Secretaries Mnuchin, Ross, Acosta; and the list goes on. The always radiant Ivanka Trump did not only a solo interview with Maria but a joint one with Mnuchin as well. In conjunction with that event, Maria also interviewed the president next door at the White House. It was a great experience and a tremendous success for the team.

The Best Breakfast Sandwich, BY TERESA

Since this story involved Secretary Mnuchin eating breakfast, let's pair it with the best breakfast sandwich. Nothing starts a day better (or cures a hangover better) than a good, hearty breakfast sandwich. This version has become a specialty in our household, since we always seem to have these ingredients on hand. The key to this stellar breakfast sandwich is the caramelized onions, which are a staple for any good burger or sandwich.

MAKES 1 SANDWICH

3 Tbsp. butter
½ medium onion, sliced
2 tsp. Worcestershire sauce or sherry vinegar
1 Tbsp. brown sugar
2 or 3 strips maple bacon
Brioche bun
2 eggs
1 slice American cheese
Mayonnaise (preferably Duke's)
Bread-and-butter pickles

Preheat the oven to 400°F. In a nonstick pan, melt the butter over low-medium heat. Once melted, add in the sliced onions and begin to cook, allowing the onions to absorb the butter. After 10 minutes, add in the Worcestershire or sherry and the brown sugar. Stir the onions well so the sauce and the sugar are distributed evenly. Turn the heat to low and allow the onions to cook until soft and caramelized.

(continued)

While the onions cook, lay a sheet of parchment paper on a sheet pan. Evenly place the uncooked bacon strips across the pan, and cook in the oven for 15 minutes. Once done, broil the bacon for 1 minute in the oven, then take it out and let it cool.

Toast the brioche bun in a separate pan over medium heat, flat side down. It should toast fairly quickly. Coat the same pan with spray cooking oil after removing the bun.

Over medium heat, cook two eggs over easy. While the eggs are cooking, prepare your bun with the mayo and pickles. After the eggs are cooked to your liking (I like to fry mine on both sides, and top with cheese to melt in the pan), assemble the sandwich with the eggs, bacon, and caramelized onions.

TO DRINK

Tequila Sunrise, BY BRIAN

This simple tropical delight will make any morning feel like a mini-vacation.

- 2 oz. tequila
- 3 oz. orange juice
- 1 dash of grenadine
- 1 healthy splash of club soda for bubbles
- 1 orange slice, for garnish
- 1 maraschino cherry, for garnish

Pour the liquid ingredients in a glass over ice, put the orange slice on the edge of the glass, and drop in the cherry.

CHAPTER 3

FaceTiming with John Daly, Zooming with Magic Johnson, Eating Jimmy Johns with Jimmy John, Mark Cuban's Opinions, Spending Time with a Terminator, and Other Strange Tales of the Paycheck Protection Program

BY BRIAN

In the spring of 2020, when the world was shutting down because of the coronavirus pandemic, the Treasury Department was tasked with implementing the Coronavirus Aid, Relief, and Economic Security (CARES) Act. Among other critical relief programs, we worked with the Small Business Administration to create the Paycheck Protection Program (PPP), which provided forgivable loans to small businesses in exchange for their keeping their employees employed. The initial funding for the program was more than $300 billion, which effectively created one of the largest financial institutions in the world out of whole cloth, and on the orders of Secretary Mnuchin, we had to create said institution in six days.

Needless to say, the dozen or so people leading this initiative did not sleep much. We worked 24/7, and the Treasury Department was one of the few places where in-person work was critical.

My job as deputy assistant secretary was, in part, to serve as the liaison to the business community and to make sure that the relief programs were working as intended, to protect as many jobs as possible. That included talking with people at banks, who had to work closely with us to disburse the loans; in the hospitality industry, which had been decimated by the pandemic; and, well, in virtually every segment of the economy.

In the course of this Herculean effort, I worked routinely with Andrew Giuliani, son of former New York City mayor Rudy Giuliani. Andrew is a great friend of mine. His father is also a great friend and former client of mine from when I was practicing law in New York before joining the administration.

Andrew was a special assistant to the president in the Office of Public Liaison at the White House. He worked his tail off, especially on matters that were important to his home state of New York. He was especially passionate about rallying support for legislation supporting 9/11 first responders.

During the time of PPP, Andrew was extremely helpful in gathering and providing feedback from the small business community. At times, this involved conversations with, shall we say, colorful figures.

On one occasion, Andrew came over to the Treasury Department for lunch in my office to discuss PPP issues. He brought Jimmy John's sandwiches. Little did I know that there was a good reason for his lunch choice, aside from the fact that Jimmy John's sandwiches are awesome.

Andrew pulled out his phone, put on the speakerphone function, and called Jimmy John Liautaud, known as JJ, the founder of Jimmy John's. As one would imagine, JJ has a wealth of knowledge about the restaurant industry, chain restaurants in particular, and was extremely helpful in explaining different business models and how relief programs could work, or not work. He is also hysterically funny and curses a blue streak. I think every other word out of his mouth that day was "f*ck." JJ was particularly pleased to know that Andrew had ordered a number seven from Jimmy John's, because that sandwich "has the best f*ckin' margins," resulting in the highest profits.

On another similar occasion, Andrew walked into my office, put his phone on my desk, and hit the speakerphone button, dialing entrepreneur Mark Cuban. I am a huge fan of *Shark Tank*, which he appears as an investor on, so this was a thrill. He shared his thoughts about PPP and how to structure relief most effectively for small businesses.

Another day, Andrew called and asked me to meet him after work down on the National Mall. He wanted to introduce me to some friends. It was a beautiful May evening, and earlier that day, the president had hosted a "Rolling to Remember" event at the White House with veterans on motorcycles honoring those missing in action or taken prisoner at war.

When I arrived, I immediately recognized the terminator, T-1000. Robert Patrick is a fantastic actor who played T-1000, Arnold Schwarzenegger's foil in *Terminator 2: Judgment Day*. It was an iconic role that everyone in my generation remembers vividly. In the movie, T-1000 killed a police officer and assumed his appearance before wreaking havoc on civilization. In real life, Robert Patrick could not have been nicer. I was interested to learn that, aside from his many acting roles, he owns a Harley Davidson dealership. He was very interested to learn that I helped to establish the Paycheck Protection Program. He had participated in the event at the White House that day, and that evening, I joined him and other veterans in continuing to honor our nation's heroes by laying a wreath at the Vietnam Veterans Memorial.

On another occasion, Andrew wasn't around, but I had a request to speak via Zoom with Magic Johnson and his team in Los Angeles about some of the issues his businesses and charitable endeavors were facing, as a result of the pandemic and the shutdowns recommended by public health authorities. I agreed, and we scheduled a meeting. When it began, I said it was an honor to speak with a living legend, and that I wished we were meeting under better circumstances. He was very kind and gracious, and we finished exchanging greetings quickly. Then, Magic explained what he was seeing and anticipating with his portfolio businesses and charities, how revenue streams were drying up, and how that affected his and his business partners' ability to provide for families in the Los Angeles area on a short, medium, and long-term basis. The conversation was brief, but it was a somber reminder of what American businesses and families across the country were facing.

It was also a subtle reminder that politics isn't always at the forefront for government officials and citizens alike. I had to talk to everybody, whether they supported President Trump or not, because we were trying to weather the crisis as a country, not as Republicans or Democrats. Magic Johnson is no supporter of Donald Trump. He is an avid Democrat who supported Hillary Clinton in 2016 and went on to support Joe Biden in 2020. Mark Cuban has a complicated relationship with President Trump, to say the least, and seemed to alternate between praising him and insulting him. Jimmy John loves Trump. None of that mattered. I had to speak with all of them—and hundreds, if not thousands, of much less famous constituents—because we were trying to save the economy in unprecedented, nearly unimaginable circumstances.

Perhaps the most memorable and insane experience in this entire period of time was speaking to golf legend John Daly.

Andrew came over to Treasury for lunch, and a group of us gathered in a newly vacated office. Geoffrey Okamoto, formerly an acting assistant secretary at the Treasury Department, had been named the new deputy managing director of the International Monetary Fund. Geoff is an amazing guy. He is kind and intelligent well beyond his thirty-five years, and so such a lofty position was well-deserved.

When Geoff departed, he vacated a beautiful and enormous office space in the Treasury Department overlooking the East Wing of the White House. Those of us left behind converted it into the Geoffrey Okamoto Memorial Lounge and Cafeteria, using his conference table to gather for meetings and lunches.

On this occasion, Andrew decided to make a call that wasn't really PPP-related. It was more of a social call. We had been working nonstop, and a few minutes of respite sounded great. So, he FaceTimed John Daly.

Daly answered from the golf course, and the conversation was everything you would dream a conversation with John Daly would be like. First, he was red-faced, smiling from ear to ear, golfing barefoot, with a cigarette hanging off his lower lip and a baseball cap on backward. Second, he cracked dirty jokes and made it clear from the get-go just how much he supported President Trump, or as John called him, "Daddy Trump." We chatted with John for a while, and then introduced him to a couple of our junior staff members, who were huge fans of his (as am I). He could not have been nicer or funnier.

In fact, he was so funny that our little group's laughter could be heard down the hall. One of the secretary's deputy chiefs of staff, Baylor Myers, was the one who heard it, and he was not pleased. I'm not sure what had gotten to Baylor that day, but he was in quite a mood. Maybe it was the stress we were all under trying to save the economy during a crisis. Maybe he'd woken up on the wrong side of the bed. Whatever it was, he was pissed.

Baylor asked me and my colleague Kaelan Dorr to step into his office. His face then became the color of a ripe tomato—also the color of the shiny red Trump tie he was wearing. He proceeded to scream at the top of his lungs, "FaceTiming with John Daly?! *During a pandemic?!*" He ranted and raved for a while, claimed we had violated some unspecified rules, and threatened to send us home, as if he were the school principal ready to call our parents. It was super weird, and also funny because Baylor was a guy in his twenties acting like a schoolmarm. I laughed at him to his face, which (surprisingly) did not make him less mad. After he got whatever was bothering him off his chest, I got on with my life and went back to work with absolutely no regrets.

When Andrew found out that we had gotten yelled at, he assumed he had been banned from the building, or at least that our lunches would have to be less fun going forward. To that, he said, "Eh, I've been banned from nicer places."

Let's be real. If you had a chance to FaceTime John Daly during your lunch break, would you do it? Of course you would. John Daly's the man.

Bourbon Vanilla French Toast, BY TERESA

This decadent version of the breakfast staple is the perfect treat for any special occasion. I made it for breakfast for Brian's thirty-ninth birthday without many cooking tools at the time. With that said, this is a fairly easy recipe that doesn't require much.

MAKES 6 SLICES

- 1 cup half-and-half
- 3 eggs
- 1 Tbsp. bourbon vanilla flavoring (Trader Joe's carries this; if you don't have it, mix 3 tsp. vanilla extract with 1 tsp. bourbon)
- 2 tsp. cinnamon
- 1 tsp. honey
- Butter
- 6 slices brioche
- Whipped cream, maple syrup, strawberries, blueberries (optional, as toppings)

Preheat the oven to 375°F. Whisk the half-and-half, eggs, bourbon vanilla flavoring, cinnamon, and honey together in a bowl. Pour into a shallow baking dish. In another baking dish, rub a stick of butter on the sides and bottom to coat.

Heat butter in a nonstick pan over medium heat. Soak each bread slice quickly in the liquid mixture on both sides, then transfer to the pan. Fry for 2 minutes on each side.

Put all slices in the buttered baking dish and bake for 5 minutes.

Carefully remove the French toast from the oven. Top with whipped cream, maple syrup, strawberries, and/or blueberries either individually or on a serving plate.

TO DRINK

John Daddy, BY BRIAN

Legendary golfer Arnold Palmer made a famous refreshing beverage that combines iced tea and lemonade. Legendary golfer—and drinker—John Daly made it acceptable to add vodka. I also cannot stop laughing at the thought of him joking around on the course about Daddy Trump. So, I've created the John Daddy in his honor.

> 3 oz. unsweetened iced tea
> 3 oz. light lemonade
> 2 oz. vodka
> Sugar or other sweetener (optional)

Pour the ingredients over ice, sweetening if desired.

CHAPTER 4

Fauci Is an Egomaniac,
but I Had a Great Day at Work

BY BRIAN

Anthony Fauci is awful. He is the highest-paid government official—so paid for his prognostications—and he always seems to be wrong. What's more, he is not just wrong. He is an arrogant, condescending politician masquerading as a learned doctor. He is lionized by the media as "America's doctor," but no one should want him to be their personal doctor, let alone America's.

At the beginning of the coronavirus pandemic in January 2020, he said the virus was nothing to worry about for the American people. Then in the months that followed, he said that people should not wear masks and that they were ineffective. By June or July, he had changed his tune and said everyone should be very concerned and that they should wear multiple masks—and goggles.

I vividly recall my blood boiling during an infuriating meeting in the Roosevelt Room of the White House, when Fauci laughed about his own goggles comment, making it clear how cynical he was and that he could get people to believe anything. He went on to laugh about how "ass-backwards" it was that people entered a restaurant wearing a mask, then sat down and conversed with people without a mask. Of course, he wasn't saying things to that effect publicly, just laughing privately at the American rubes he was fooling.

I will never forget that when Operation Warp Speed (the vaccine manufacturing plan) was getting underway in the spring and summer of 2020, Fauci said we couldn't possibly make a vaccine in fewer than eighteen months. Operation Warp Speed did it in nine months. (So close. Fauci was off by only 100 percent!) President Trump and his team had created a plan to both test and manufacture vaccines simultaneously to dramatically cut the time it would take to get them to market, and it worked.

Then there was a real kicker for me as a communications staffer. In October 2020, Fauci went on *60 Minutes*, one of the highest-rated shows on television—dressed in a black turtleneck and tweed jacket like some sort of tortured poet—and said, without a hint of irony, that the White House staff was silencing him. On *60 Minutes*. As the kids would say on Twitter—let that sink in. In that interview, Fauci also blamed President Trump for the fact that Trump had contracted COVID-19. This was a segment during which CBS aired B-roll footage of the octogenarian Fauci power-walking in spandex with a security detail. I say this to underscore just how ridiculous this person is.

This is all incredibly frustrating. But wait, there's more!

In December 2020, Fauci went on a cable news program where he was asked whether President Trump should be vaccinated, even though he had recovered from COVID-19 recently. Fauci said he would recommend that the president get vaccinated. Virtually all other doctors—including the president's own physicians—had advised that he should not get the shot yet because he had antibodies from his recent recovery. In other words, Fauci was wrong again. He just said what he thought the cable news anchor wanted to hear.

Finally, one other note about Operation Warp Speed: In addition to claiming that it could not possibly work, Fauci fought against it tooth and nail. During the course of the clinical trials, he frequently asked manufacturers to lengthen them, add more people, add more diversity, and do essentially anything and everything to slow down the process. I know this because he told us this in task force meetings—that even when there were more than thirty thousand participants, he insisted on forty or forty-five thousand. He even advocated for specifically recruiting more "latinx" into the trials. (Latinx is a term to describe people of Latin American decent, and polling data indicates that Latino and Hispanic people find it offensive.) And yet, in March 2021, he appeared to take credit for Warp Speed, saying it "was the best decision" *he* had "ever made."

Of course, you're not supposed to say any of this. After all, according to Fauci, to criticize him is to criticize "science itself," which he said in June 2021.

Truly, this man has no shame. What a boob. Or to paraphrase how some colleagues referred to him, that "tyrannical, snaky little garden gnome."

During the 2020 campaign, President Trump summed up the White House staff's relationship with Fauci pretty well with public comments. He said that Fauci threw bombs whenever he went on TV, but it would be a "bigger bomb" if the president moved to pull him off the air or fire him altogether. Because of the media's hero worship of Fauci, he enjoyed very high approval numbers during the campaign. And so, the choice was between letting this guy run his mouth or bracing for a brutal firestorm. Sometimes in life, there are only bad choices. This was one of those times.

Anyway, it feels good to get that off my chest, but this story is regarding a particular episode of Fauci egomania.

Historically, the president of the United States has often been invited to throw out the first pitch for the opening day of Major League Baseball. In 2020, MLB planned to invite President Trump. At least, that is the intention they had signaled to us.

Lo and behold, while arrangements were being made between the White House and MLB to have Trump throw out the first pitch, the Washington Nationals issued a press release stating that Fauci would throw out the first pitch. You see, the Nationals owners are Democrats and friends of Fauci's. And they and their friend Fauci believed that, even though Fauci was somewhere south of Antarctica on the government org chart, actually he was more important than the president. (Fauci reported to the National Institutes of Health director, who reported to a deputy secretary, who reported to the secretary of Health and Human Services, who reported to the president.)

Needless to say, it was an awkward situation. But there was some good news. First, poetic justice prevailed. Fauci threw out the first pitch, but it landed about halfway between the mound and the first-base-side dugout—nowhere even remotely close to home plate—which was just embarrassing on a historic scale. Aside from Carly Rae Jepsen spiking the ball directly into the ground, it might have been the worst pitch ever thrown.

The other great bit of news for me was that while the president would have been happy to throw out the first pitch, he actually didn't care very much about the scheduling snafu—so we organized an Opening Day event at the White House.

Andrew Giuliani has a great friendship with one of the greatest (and one of my favorite) players in the history of baseball, retired Yankees pitcher and Hall of Famer Mariano Rivera. Andrew invited him to the White House along with a gaggle of Little Leaguers to play catch and chat with President Trump to celebrate the beginning of the baseball season.

It was a perfect day with hardly a cloud in the sky, and everyone had a smile from ear to ear. I even got a chance to spend a few minutes chatting with Mariano in White House press secretary Kayleigh McEnany's office.

Just days prior, my brother, John, had given me a copy of *Time* magazine that he had found while going through boxes of old stuff at our family's house. It was from 1998, when the Yankees had just won their third consecutive World Series title. Right there on the cover was Mariano in the middle of a pile of Yankees celebrating their big win. I showed it to Mariano, and I could tell he was moved. He said it reminded him of the "pure joy" they had felt that day. Of course, I got him to sign it for me, and it hangs in my office to this day, just as it hung in my White House office after that day.

That day after our baseball event concluded, Andrew and I helped to execute an idea we had been trying to bring to fruition, but which had thus far proven elusive. We got Dave Portnoy, the founder of Barstool Sports, to visit the White House and interview President Trump.

With apologies for the baseball metaphor, the interview was a home run. If you haven't watched it, you should. This discussion was not a news interview. It was not what people were used to. It was different. It was conversational. It was two interesting people talking about interesting things (with the White House Rose Garden as the backdrop). They talked about sports, the president's life as a celebrity before entering politics and, of course, the trouble Trump often got into because of Twitter—almost always because of the retweets, the president said.

Following the interview, a group of us filtered into the Oval Office and sat on the couches. The president and Mariano autographed some commemorative items together, and the Barstool staff took pictures with President Trump at the Resolute desk. I sat next to counselor to the president Hope Hicks and deputy chief of staff Dan Scavino and said to them, "We get paid to do this? Like, this is our job?" They laughed.

As we were all wrapping up our mini love fest in the Oval, we agreed that the next move was to get Dave to do a review of the pizza made by the chef on Air Force One. I suppose we just ran out of time, but to this day, I am furious that we never made this happen.

In any event, this was probably the best day at work I've ever had, and it might be the best day at work I ever will have. As the great Larry David would say, it was pretty pretty pretty pretty pretty good.

Opening-Day Burgers, BY BRIAN

MAKES 7 PATTIES, EACH ABOUT 5 OZ. AND 1¼ INCHES THICK

2 lbs. Wagyu ground beef, preferably 85% lean, formed into 7 patties
1 cup Worcestershire sauce
1 cup balsamic vinegar
¼ cup garlic salt
7 brioche buns
7 slices American cheese
Bread-and-butter chip pickles
Butter lettuce
1 tomato, sliced
1 white onion, sliced
Mayonnaise

Put the patties in an 8-by-11-inch glass dish. Pour the Worcestershire sauce over the patties until it's about a quarter of the way up their sides. Add the balsamic vinegar until the mixture is about halfway up the sides. Sprinkle garlic salt on one side of each patty, reserving at least half of it for the other sides.

Cover the dish with plastic wrap and put it in the refrigerator overnight.

In the morning, flip the patties and sprinkle garlic salt on the other sides. Let the patties sit in the sauce for a few more hours until you're ready to cook them.

Heat a grill to 400°F degrees or, if using a grill pan, heat it over medium-high heat. Put the patties on the grill or pan; if using a grill, close the lid. Cook them for about 4 minutes. Flip them and close the lid for another

3 minutes. Open the lid and let the patties cook for about 2 more minutes. If you're using a meat thermometer, you want them to be between 140° and 150° F for medium-cooked burgers with pink in the middle. Note that the intensity of grills and cooktops, and personal preferences, can vary quite dramatically—some degree of judgment is involved here to make sure your meat is cooked thoroughly and to your liking. Toast the buns on the grill and melt the American cheese on each patty for about 45 seconds.

Take the buns off the grill and put the patties on the buns. Add the pickles, lettuce, tomato, and white onions on top of the patties. (Pro tip: For excellent caramelized onions, use Teresa's method from the Best Breakfast Sandwich recipe in chapter two.)

Spread mayo or Miracle Whip on the top bun, and/or put on the side for dipping.

TO DRINK

Beer Selection, BY BRIAN

Sometimes the perfect drink is a beer. Wild Acre Brewing Company's Agave Americana is an excellent, refreshing, light, and summery beer. I also must say, though, that the Germans really know their beer. Some of Teresa's and my favorites include a crisp Spaten Lager, a Radeberger Pilsner, or a classic Hofbräu Hefe Weizen. We won't judge you if you drink it out of a giant glass boot.

CHAPTER 5

First Solo Trip with President Trump

BY BRIAN

It was the weekend of August 8, 2020. The prior month, I had been named White House deputy press secretary and deputy communications director. I had gotten my feet under me for a few weeks, and Press Secretary Kayleigh McEnany was sending me on my first trip to staff the president alone. It was supposed to be an easy mission. We were going to his golf club in Bedminster, New Jersey, and a fundraiser in the Hamptons on Long Island, New York. We didn't expect there to be any events that were open to the press, so it was a chance for me to spend some additional time with the press corps, members of the senior staff, some supporters and friends, and the president.

I arrived at the staff hotel about ten minutes away from the golf club. I changed into khakis and a polo shirt, which I figured would be appropriate for the club, and headed over.

I had just arrived at the club and was getting the lay of the land when my phone buzzed. It was Kayleigh. I answered, thinking maybe there was a reporter she wanted me to talk to, or perhaps was just checking in to make sure I had made it on-site. I was wrong.

She said, "The president wants to do a news conference." I said, "Okay, when?" She said, "An hour or less."

I was off to the races. I went over to the clubhouse, where the event would take place. I scanned the room and spoke with the advance staff. The cameras were getting set up, and I checked to see what the camera shot would look like. I also worked with the digital team on the graphics that would be displayed on the monitors near the podium. Finally, I spoke with Gaby Hurt, our press wrangler, to make sure the press corps would be ushered into the room quickly.

On each trip, we take a wrangler. Wranglers are typically junior press office staff members whose job it is to babysit the press corps and make sure they are logistically supported. For example, when the president calls a news conference, the wrangler works with the advance staff and Secret Service to escort the reporters to the location.

Then I began reviewing the latest news and Twitter, and had one or two casual off-the-record conversations with reporters to gauge what was on their minds and try to predict what they would ask the president.

The big news of the day was a report published by the head of counterintelligence in the Office of the Director of National Intelligence. The head of counterintelligence was William (Bill) Evanina, and his report was focused on our adversaries' election interference activities, and their preferred candidates in the upcoming election. The report stated that China preferred Joe Biden over Trump, Russia preferred Trump over Biden, and Iran was mainly seeking to undermine America's institutions but certainly opposed a second term for Trump, given his administration's pressure on the regime.

I knew the press would zero in on the Russia part and ignore the other two countries. They had been obsessed with Russia for years and had convinced themselves that Trump was somehow a Russian plant, in spite of a complete lack of any evidence and the fact that his administration had implemented the most aggressive sanctions ever against Russia.

I wanted to make sure the president was prepared for a question on it. I had a great relationship with the director of National Intelligence, John Ratcliffe, because he and I had discussed having me serve on his front office staff. That was before I wound up at the White House, but we remained friendly when I did go. So, I called Ratcliffe and let him know that the president was going to do a news conference, and that I was sure he would get a question about the counterintelligence report. We discussed possible responses, and his excellent recommendation was to focus on the fact that it was no surprise that our adversaries were trying to disrupt our elections because of how strong our foreign policy was, and how disruptive our administration had been to those who wanted to see the decline of our country. The president had implemented the harshest ever sanctions on Iran and Russia, overseen the demise of Iranian terrorist and general Qasem Soleimani, and renegotiated trade with China to address China's unfair practices, to name a few noteworthy items.

By that point, the president was in a dining room behind the ballroom where the press conference would take place. He sat with a small group of staff going over some prepared remarks that he would use at the beginning of the event. Dan Scavino, one of the president's closest and longest-serving aides, had been with the president but stepped out of the room briefly. I saw him in the hallway and told him that I wanted to make sure the president was prepared for a question that I knew was coming.

So he said, "Okay, go in and talk to him." So I did.

I walked into the room. I quickly realized that I was the only one without a suit on. That made sense. This was the president of the United States preparing to do a news conference, after all. I felt pretty stupid.

President Trump didn't miss a beat. He looked at the logo on my red polo shirt, which was a black "G," and said, "Green Bay Packers?" I said, "Georgia Bulldogs." He said, "Even better," and we all had a laugh.

Teresa is a University of Georgia alumna, and her folks had given me the shirt when they took me to my first Georgia football game. In fairness to the president, the Georgia "G" and the Green Bay "G" look pretty much exactly alike.

We moved on quickly from the small talk and started talking about the intelligence issue, as well as a variety of other news stories, as the president reviewed his prepared remarks. I passed along Ratcliffe's thoughts on the report and how to handle questions.

When the president felt ready, he called for someone to get him the phone with his Twitter account, because he wanted to tweet that he would be doing a news conference shortly.

When he had the smartphone, he held it out in front of him, tilted his head upward, and looked down over the end of his nose at the screen. He began typing with his pointer finger in a hunt-and-peck fashion. He looked up at me and said, "No other president would do this. You think other administrations did it this way? Nobody else does this." I laughed and agreed. He hit send on a tweet giving a few minutes' warning that he would be starting his press conference.

This was a big reason why he had become the president in the first place. He spoke directly to his constituents without a filter. I always laughed when journalists would start to complain that Trump was not transparent for whatever reason. You could accuse Donald Trump of a lot of things, and the press still does, but a lack of transparency is not one of them. His thoughts on everything from foreign policy to celebrity couples were put out there for the world to see.

Before heading to the ballroom, the president called to a member of the golf club staff and asked that members of the club be allowed into the back of the room to watch the news conference. The members quickly lined the back wall with drinks in hand and enormous smiles on their faces. (Of course, some joyless reporter tried to dox them and shame them on Twitter for not wearing masks.)

When he was ready, the president walked out to the area behind the curtain to prepare to enter the news conference. As was custom, he had a mirror and supplies to freshen up, including TRESemmé hairspray.

Then he walked out and began the news conference. He read his prepared remarks. When he concluded those, he received several questions, one of which was the one I predicted about foreign adversaries and our elections. It came from Reuters. As predicted, the question was only focused on Russia. The president took it head-on and asked why the reporter was focused only on Russia and not the other two countries. He went on to say that he believed "nobody's been tougher on Russia than I have, ever," adding that China would love it if he lost to Joe Biden because then "they would own our country."

It was a strong answer, but a different answer received the strongest reaction from everyone in the room. One of the reporters asked about the members of the club in the back of the room without masks on. The president replied, "It's a peaceful protest." It brought the house down with laughter from the members and outrage from the press.

For months, cities across America had experienced extremely violent protests organized by various left-wing organizations, including Antifa and Black Lives Matter. In spite of social distancing guidelines and various other concerns about the coronavirus, mainstream reporters seemed unconcerned about these types of gatherings. However, they were always very concerned when groups of Trump supporters got together.

When lefties gathered, the press reported on "peaceful protests," including when police stations were burned to the ground, statues of the founding fathers were toppled and defaced, and business owners were looted and put out of work. A CNN personality infamously reported on a "fiery but mostly peaceful" protest directly in front of a burning building during a riot. But when more than one Trump supporter arrived in the same space, routine events magically morphed into murderous "super-spreader" events.

These are the rules, apparently.

The president did well at his press conference. The reporters got spicy quotes and interesting stories, and he had fun. It was a heck of a way for me, as a staffer, to start the weekend.

After that press conference, I had an incredible experience. We had a relatively slow weekend, compared to some others, in terms of news coverage, and I was able to travel with the team to the president's fund-raising events on Long Island.

For mere mortals, the trip from Bedminster to the Hamptons in the summer, typically, would be brutal. You would have to drive at least three hours sitting in stop-and-go traffic, starting in the middle of New Jersey and going across the George Washington Bridge; through parts of Manhattan, the Bronx, and Queens; and then all the way out to the edge of the world in the Hamptons.

This particular trip involved helicopters and a motorcade. I don't remember exactly how long it took, but my guess is about thirty to forty minutes. We took a quick trip to an open field in New Jersey, where we boarded helicopters. The president flew on Marine One. I joined other staff members on a Boeing V-22 Osprey, where we watched clouds float by the open back of the chopper. We landed in a field near an elementary school and hopped in a motorcade to the first event.

This was my first time in a presidential motorcade. It is an experience unlike any other. Basically, there's no such thing as traffic lights, only the lights of the vehicles in front of you and behind you. People lined the streets for miles and miles—in residential Long Island neighborhoods, in one of the bluest states in the country—waving Trump flags, cheering, and taking pictures. It was fun. I thought, "I could get used to this."

Since the fundraising events were private, I won't get into details except to say that the audiences were obviously supportive, and the hospitality was extremely gracious.

The way back to Bedminster was just as cool, maybe better. This time our helicopter ride was in the evening overlooking the lights of Manhattan and the Statue of Liberty.

As a former New Yorker, I still can't get over the fact that I was flying with the president of the United States over the skyline, and it happened to be the president who had his name on buildings in that very skyline.

Clubhouse Steak Sandwich, BY TERESA

President Trump famously loves steak, and Brian had steak for dinner when he was in Bedminster, so it's only fitting that we pair this story with a delicious steak dish—my famous steak sandwich with caramelized onions and horseradish aioli. It's a crowd pleaser!

MAKES 1 SANDWICH

¼ cup mayonnaise
1 garlic clove, smashed into a paste
1½ Tbsp. fresh horseradish
1 tsp. lemon juice
Butter
1 shallot, sliced
½ medium onion, sliced
2 tsp. brown sugar
2 tsp. Champagne vinegar
2 beef tenderloin medallions
Salt and pepper to taste
Truffle butter (optional)
2 slices sourdough bread, thickly sliced
1 cup arugula

Begin by making the horseradish aioli. Mix the mayo, garlic, horseradish, and lemon juice until blended. Add salt and pepper to taste. Refrigerate while cooking the rest of the meal.

In a nonstick pan, heat the butter over medium heat. Once melted, add in the shallots and onion and begin to cook to soften. Halfway, add in the brown sugar and Champagne vinegar. Turn the heat to low and cook for another 10 minutes or until the shallots and onion are opaque and soft.

Next, season the beef medallions with salt and pepper on both sides. In a grill pan, heat a tablespoon of butter over high heat. Once the butter is melted and the pan is hot, cook the steaks about 4 to 5 minutes on each side or an internal temperature of 135°F for medium, depending on the thickness of the meat. Optional to finish with truffle butter for a special kick. Allow to rest for about 5 minutes after cooking. Slice thinly.

Toast slices of sourdough either in the pan where you cooked the steaks or in the toaster. Slather a layer of the horseradish aioli on each slice of bread. Then add the sliced steak, followed by a layer of the caramelized onions. Top with arugula and close the sandwich. It is truly a decadent dish!

Manhattan Helo Ride, BY BRIAN

You can't have a story involving a helicopter ride over Manhattan and not pair it with a Manhattan. This drink is a classic. I've just softened it a bit because I prefer a bit of citrus, sweet spiciness, and a few bubbles.

- 2 oz. bourbon
- 1 oz. dry vermouth (I've had Manhattan connoisseurs tell me sweet vermouth is better, but I've made it with dry vermouth and enjoyed it.)
- 2 dashes of Angostura bitters
- 1 dash of orange bitters
- 1 oz. ginger ale
- 1 orange twist
- 1 maraschino cherry

Put ice in a shaker and add the bourbon, vermouth, and bitters. Shake well. Strain into a cocktail glass. Pour in the ginger ale. Stir. Twist the orange rind over the glass and then hang it on the rim. Drop in the cherry and serve.

Heaven and Angels Sing, BY TERESA

We enjoyed the steak sandwich during the Christmas season with this drink, which I've named for the classic tune "Hark the Herald Angels Sing." Why pair a great meal with one drink when you can have two?

> 1 bottle Champagne or prosecco
> 1 bottle elderflower lemonade
> 1 jar maraschino cherries

Pour two parts Champagne and one part elderflower lemonade into a Champagne glass. Add 1 cherry and swirl in a bit of the cherry syrup to give the drink a light red color.

CHAPTER 6

Jon Voight Wanted to Plan Our Wedding

BY TERESA

One of the coolest perks of working in the Pentagon's Public Affairs division was getting a behind-the-scenes look at how movie and television show creators work with the Department of Defense to create epic depictions of the U.S. military, both past and present. The office tasked with that job has a multitude of resources and connections to keep the public informed and engaged with the military through several avenues, including nonprofits serving the veteran community.

In 2020, COVID-19 was impacting the country during the same year that the nation was celebrating the seventy-fifth anniversary of the end of World War II. It was a monumental milestone, and the Pentagon, along with several other federal agencies and the White House, was planning to hold incredible celebrations to honor those who had served and sacrificed during that historic time. It also would be one of the last chances to celebrate the Greatest Generation. There were so few survivors of that generation still alive, as so many had left us due to old age.

The impact of COVID was a huge blow to those plans, so the Pentagon's Public Affairs office had to scramble to do something memorable in a safe way. The people we wanted to celebrate were the prime types at risk of getting COVID and suffering severe effects. One of my colleagues, Captain Morgan Murphy, came up with a brilliant idea to do a thirty-minute movie-quality program highlighting several veterans of the war—from nurses to paratroopers. In addition to highlighting the service of a veteran in each section of the video, a celebrity would introduce and meet with that person. The planning behind this program took a team effort, but the end result was a beautiful tribute to those who had served.

We got in touch with several amazing veterans, all of whom were not scared of COVID at all! Most were happy to make the trip to D.C. to film and share their incredibly touching stories. In mid-August, we paired one lovely veteran with legendary actor Jon Voight for a day of filming. The star of films ranging from *Midnight Cowboy* to *Deliverance* to *Pearl Harbor* to *National Treasure*, and on and on, Jon is one of the greatest and most recognizable actors of multiple generations. And perhaps more importantly, he is a patriot. So he did not hesitate one bit to travel to D.C. on his own dime and lend his support to our project.

It was an absolute delight to work with him. You could tell how much it meant to him, and how much he enjoyed spending time with our veteran, an amazing man named Linc Harner, and hearing his war stories.

Linc had served in the Army during World War II. He recalled hearing of the bombing of Pearl Harbor and President Roosevelt's "Day of Infamy" speech when he was in high school. He enlisted in the Army to fight on behalf of our country, and he stormed the beaches of Normandy to help win the war. At one point, while listening to Linc talk about his love of our country, Jon shed a few tears. You don't see that kind of pride much anymore, especially in our divided society.

While we were in awe of Linc, we also still couldn't believe that an A-list celebrity was taking so much time out of his day to spend it with us. After filming, all of us including Jon agreed to go celebrate our successful filming day at the Trump Hotel in D.C. We found a comfortable couch and some chairs at the lobby bar and restaurant, where those of us on the Public Affairs staff shared our stories of how we had gotten to the Pentagon. Brian joined us as well; he had just had the pleasure of speaking with Jon a few weeks before at the White House. Jon was especially interested in speaking with Brian, given that the election was heating up and Brian had a front-row seat to all the action in the West Wing.

While I was enjoying my favorite drink, a French 75, Brian and I started speaking with Jon about how we met and our relationship. He listened intently, almost intensely, and with enthusiasm. It was crystal clear that this was a man who loved love. After he asked us some questions, and we answered them, he had heard enough. He had a plan for us. He said, "I think you should go to the Boar's Head Inn this weekend and get married!" The Boar's Head Inn is a resort a couple of hours south of Washington, D.C., and Jon loved the place. Brian and I looked at each other and smiled, then we laughed.

I could tell that the wheels in Brian's head were turning. Brian thanked Jon for the suggestion, but we did not, in fact, run away and get married that weekend. However, only three weeks later, Brian did take me on a trip up to the Omni Homestead in Hot Springs, Virginia, where he proposed and I said yes! I think Jon Voight had a huge part in influencing that decision.

We will never forget the time we spent with him and our colleagues, making fun memories despite all the worries about COVID happening in the world. Jon Voight restored some of our faith in humanity, showing us that someone could be so successful and a cultural icon, and remain a genuine, loving, and patriotic person.

French Onion Quiche, BY TERESA

This heartwarming story deserves a warm and decadent dish. Everyone loves a bowl of good French onion soup. I also love eggs. This recipe takes the foundational flavors of French onion soup and turns the soup into a warm quiche. It's absolutely delicious and elevates the traditional quiche into a special breakfast—or any meal, really.

MAKES 1 PIE, SERVES 8

2 Tbsp. butter
1 medium onion, sliced
¼ cup sherry vinegar
1 Tbsp. brown sugar
1½ cup mushrooms (cremini or shiitake, or both)
1 tsp. thyme
Salt and pepper to taste
1 cup half-and-half
2 large eggs
1 Tbsp. garlic powder
1½ cup Gruyère, shredded
1½ cup Swiss cheese, shredded
1 frozen pie crust

Preheat the oven to 350°F. In a pan, heat the butter on low-medium heat. When the butter is melted, add in the onions and cook for 5 minutes. Add in the sherry vinegar and brown sugar and cook on low heat for another 5 minutes. Add in the mushrooms, thyme, salt, and pepper to taste and cook for another 5 minutes until the onions are caramelized and the mushrooms are soft. Cool the mixture for 5 minutes after it is done.

While the onions and mushrooms are cooking, combine the half-and-half, eggs, and garlic powder in a bowl. Whisk together until the custard mixture is smooth.

Place the frozen pie crust on a baking sheet and pour in a small amount of the custard mixture. Then layer in some of the onion-and-mushroom mixture over the custard. Top with some of the shredded Gruyère and Swiss cheese. Repeat until the ingredients fill the pie crust to the edge, ending with Gruyère and Swiss cheeses on the top.

Bake in the oven for 35 to 40 minutes, until the cheese forms a golden brown crust. Remove and let the quiche cool for 30 minutes. Serve for breakfast, lunch, or dinner!

Tip: Instead of washing the mushrooms in a bowl of water, rub any dirt off them with a wet paper towel. This prevents the mushrooms from soaking up too much water and watering down the dish.

Trenchie 75, by Teresa and Brian

This is Teresa's favorite drink, which she had that evening with Jon Voight! It's a twist on a French 75. When we went to Paris, Teresa not only had a French 75 there, we also loved the restaurant Frenchie. So we call this the Trenchie 75.

2 oz. vodka
1 oz. St. Germain elderflower liqueur
1 tsp. simple syrup
1 tsp. lemon juice
3 oz. Champagne
1 lemon twist

Put a few crushed ice cubes in a shaker. Add the vodka, St. Germain, simple syrup, and lemon juice. Shake well. Strain into a glass. Top with the Champagne and lemon twist.

CHAPTER 7

Discussing the "Tiger King" on Air Force One

BY BRIAN

On August 18, 2020, President Trump boarded Air Force One for a trip to Iowa. White House press secretary Kayleigh McEnany and I, among other staff, joined him. As was customary, if issues arose during the flight warranting public statements, or at least a discussion, one or both of us would walk up to the front of the plane to the president's cabin to speak with him. There were a variety of serious issues on the agenda that day, including an event regarding disaster recovery in Iowa and an immigration speech in Arizona. However, one question seemed to keep coming up in casual conversation—among White House staff, journalists, and at what seemed from our vantage point to be every proverbial water cooler in America: Should President Trump grant a pardon to Joe Exotic, the "Tiger King"?

Joseph Maldonado Passage, aka Joe Exotic or the Tiger King, had captured America's attention at the beginning of the coronavirus pandemic when a Netflix documentary about him shot to the top of the charts. Exotic was convicted on animal cruelty charges relating to a tiger zoo that he was operating and his role in a failed murder-for-hire scheme targeting his rival, the now-infamous Carole Baskin (who some suspect of killing her husband and feeding him to tigers).

Around this time, it seemed like people could not stop discussing whether Exotic should have been found guilty at all, whether his twenty-two-year prison sentence was too harsh, and whether Baskin was guilty or innocent regarding her husband's disappearance.

On one occasion, I recall walking in front of the White House North Portico on my way to the Treasury Department next door—a trip I had made countless times. Secret Service agents spaced about thirty yards apart were dutifully watching the passersby on the street while exchanging thoughts about all things Tiger King—including Baskin. I couldn't help but participate. I yelled to both of them: "So, she totally fed her husband to the tigers, right?" One agent exclaimed: "Ah, yup!" while the other yelled, "Oh, absolutely—this guy gets it!" Then we all laughed, felt a little uncomfortable, and went on with our day.

Anyway, so there we were sitting in the president's cabin on Air Force One. President Trump and his chief of staff, Mark Meadows, were having a conversation at the desk, and Kayleigh and I were sitting on the couch. Kayleigh and I were discussing the pros and cons of tweeting a tiger emoji with no other commentary, and the likely scale of the ensuing internet meltdown. Then the president and Meadows started to pay attention to our conversation.

Trump had been asked about the Tiger King by a reporter in recent days and admitted that he hadn't watched the show. But, he said, he'd "look at" whether he should issue a pardon. Meadows was not very familiar with the situation either and asked what it was all about. Kayleigh and I explained.

"Well, you see, Joe Exotic is a tiger zoo owner in Oklahoma who keeps running for office," I began. When Exotic had run for office, he'd given out condoms with his face on them. Luckily, I didn't get to that part in this conversation. Kayleigh jumped in saying, "And he's known as the Tiger King. He was convicted of this murder-for-hire scheme, and people keep asking if you're going to pardon him." Meadows had heard enough with "murder-for-hire" and said abruptly, "Yeah, that doesn't sound like something we ought to be involved with." With that, he and the president returned to their conversation about more pressing matters, and Kayleigh and I turned our attention to various stories we were monitoring in the press.

Thinking back on it, while it wasn't under any sort of serious consideration, I wish I had asked one more time for President Trump's take on the matter, because his entertaining, one-of-a-kind thoughts and quips on bizarre cultural phenomena have helped him become one of the most famous human beings in the history of the world. Alas, we went back to doing the serious business of the American people.

Stir-Fry, BY TERESA

In a story about Joe Exotic, we should have a recipe that's a little exotic. When I was growing up, my mother made many Korean dishes for me. I feel very lucky to have been exposed to so many different flavors and foods. Korean food is my version of comfort food. This stir-fry is super easy, and I've put a little Korean twist on it. You can source Korean spices and foods at many grocery stores these days, and you can certainly find them at international food markets.

SERVES 4

1 tsp. sesame oil

3 Tbsp. soy sauce

2 tsp. rice vinegar

1 Tbsp. gochujang paste

3 tsp. brown sugar

Olive oil

2 cloves garlic, minced

2 green onions, sliced horizontally, green and white parts separated

2 tsp. ginger, minced (fresh preferred)

½ lb. uncooked shrimp

¼ cup shredded carrots

2 bulbs baby bok choy, leaves separated

½ cup sliced shiitake mushrooms

Rice, noodles, quinoa, or other grain, for serving

Sesame seeds, for garnish

Optional: top with crushed peanuts and/or cilantro for added texture and flavor

In a bowl, whisk together the sesame oil, soy sauce, rice vinegar, gochujang, and brown sugar to make a marinade. Let it sit while the other ingredients cook, whisking again before adding it to the cooked ingredients.

In a nonstick pan over medium heat, heat a layer of olive oil. Add in the garlic, white part of the green onions, and ginger, and cook until fragrant. Next, add the shrimp and cook until pink. Remove the shrimp and place in a separate bowl.

In the same pan, add in the carrots, bok choy, and mushrooms, and cook over medium heat. Whisk the marinade thoroughly and add it to the mixture. Then add the shrimp back into the pan and stir to combine all the ingredients. Cook for 5 more minutes. Serve over a bed of rice, noodles, quinoa, or other grain of your choice, and garnish with sesame seeds, and peanuts and/or cilantro.

TO DRINK

Asian Pear Martini, BY TERESA AND BRIAN

Enjoy with extreme caution—seriously, no driving or operating heavy machinery after this one. It is delicious and strong!

 1 oz. sake
 1 oz. vodka
 1 oz. pear liquor
 1 oz. apple juice
 1 slice Asian pear

Put ice in a shaker. Add all ingredients except the pear slice. Shake well. Strain into a cocktail glass. Add the pear slice to the rim.

CHAPTER 8

There Have Been 45 Presidents but There Has Been Only One Jack Nicklaus

BY BRIAN

Many Americans might not realize that the president has several planes, not just one, and whichever one he is on carries the call sign Air Force One. Without getting into too many details, generally speaking he takes either a big plane or a small plane, and which plane he takes depends on the size of the airport runway. The big plane is a 747, and it requires a longer runway to land than the smaller plane does.

In case you're wondering, the small plane is nice, but the big plane is way better. It's roomier, the conference room is nicer, the president's office space is much bigger, and the staff areas are more comfortable.

Anyway, on one of the trips I took with the president, we were on a small plane. Several of us were sitting in the conference room behind President Trump's office. I saw something move out of the corner of my eye and realized it was the president turning the corner from his office and coming back towards us. During flights, he frequently came out to chat with the staff and tell stories.

Sometimes he would also go back to the press cabin to chat with the press corps. On my favorite such occasion (not this occasion), he asked me for the list of reporters on the plane with us. I always kept a copy handy in case he asked. I handed him the list, and as he normally did, he looked it over, smirked at a few of the names, and commented that there were "some real beauties," a term he used to refer to the worst of the worst.

Then he asked me if I thought he should go back and talk to the "fake news" people. He didn't wait for a response. He just smiled and blurted out, "Let's go talk to these fake f*cks," and darted past me towards the press cabin. I leaped out of my chair and followed him. He had a perfectly cordial, mostly off-the-record session with the reporters, and we returned to the front of the plane. This anecdote is a perfect encapsulation of how even though the press treated President Trump poorly, which everyone knows, he never shied away from them. In fact, he quite enjoyed sparring with them.

Anyway, on this other occasion, Trump was telling stories to the staff. He brought up one of the times he'd played golf with Jack Nicklaus. Of course, Nicklaus is arguably the greatest golfer of all time, having won 117 professional tournaments and eighteen majors. The president asked us whether we thought it was harder to be president or harder to do what Jack Nicklaus had done. Staff Secretary Derek Lyons was quick to reply that being president of the United States was harder. President Trump smirked, shrugged, and said, "I don't know. Eighteen majors. I mean, come on. There have been forty-five presidents. There's only one Jack." Hard to argue with that.

TO EAT

All-Time Greatest Turkey Burgers, BY TERESA

As an alternative (or supplement) to Brian's beef burgers, these turkey burgers are a great, lighter summertime cookout dish. They're excellent grilled, and the cilantro and garlic give it a really interesting flavor kick.

MAKES 6 PATTIES

2 packs (about 2 to 2½ lbs.) ground turkey
½ yellow onion, finely chopped
2 Tbsp. cilantro, chopped
1 Tbsp. garlic salt
1 Tbsp. garlic marinade (Garlic Expressions preferred)
1½ Tbsp. Worcestershire sauce
1 Tbsp. balsamic vinegar
1 egg yolk
6 brioche buns
Mayonnaise
Dijon mustard
Lettuce
Bread-and-butter chip pickles

Place the ground turkey in a bowl, and then add in all of the ingredients (except the mayo, mustard, lettuce, and pickles). Using your hands, combine the ingredients. Let the meat soak up the marinade. If you have time, cover the dish and let it sit in the refrigerator for an hour or so. Then pack the meat into six individual patties.

These are great to cook on the grill or the stovetop. Make sure they cook through thoroughly, usually at least 4 minutes on each side, until the patties reach an internal temperature of 165°F. We usually serve them on brioche buns with mayo, Dijon mustard, lettuce, and bread and butter chip pickles.

The Golden Gentleman, BY BRIAN

One of the simplest and most delicious drinks around is a whiskey and ginger ale. I've just classed it up a bit by adding a hint of lime and named it in honor of perhaps the greatest golfer or sportsman ever—the "Golden Bear," Jack Nicklaus.

2 oz. whiskey (Gentleman Jack preferred)
3 oz. ginger ale
½ oz. lime juice
Lime wedge, for garnish

Pour all the ingredients except the lime wedge in a glass over ice and stir. Add the lime wedge to the rim for garnish.

CHAPTER 9

When You're Right Above the Gift Shop

BY TERESA

"Coffee?" That was the question every morning as soon as I walked into my office in the Eisenhower Executive Office Building (EEOB), right next to the West Wing of the White House. My colleague and now close friend Ninio Fetalvo would ask that question before our morning meeting with Jared Kushner and a select group of COVID-19 task force members and staff.

Jared is an incredible person and one of the most effective members of the administration. His energy, organizational capabilities, negotiating skill, and focus were responsible for some monumental accomplishments. He was a driving force behind the Abraham Accords, which led to normalized relations between Israel and several Arab nations, and he was a voice of reason and drive when it came to keeping Operation Warp Speed on the right path for approving and distributing vaccines.

I will never forget a morning meeting leading into the Thanksgiving holiday weekend. Senior officials from the FDA were on the conference line with those of us who were in the room. We were always eager to hear about any progress on approving treatments and vaccine candidates. The

FDA, of course, is notoriously bureaucratic and typically takes years to evaluate and approve products. We didn't have that kind of time because over one thousand people per day were dying at least in part because of the coronavirus.

On this particular day, Jared made exactly that point. He asked the FDA officials a simple question. He wanted to know, while these critical evaluations were pending, "Are the people working on this taking the Thanksgiving break?" There was silence on the other end of the phone. He added, "A thousand people a day are dying." The point was received. He didn't belabor it and moved on to the next agenda item, but just by asking the question, he had made a powerful statement.

I digress. This story is not nearly so serious. The coffee shop in EEOB was conveniently located one floor below us. It was just a quick jaunt down the historic spiral stairs right outside our office. We loved going and getting our coffee cards stamped (buy nine coffees and the tenth one was free!).

Also conveniently located near the coffee shop was the White House Gift Shop run by the Navy Mess staff. (The Navy Mess is the name of the dining room in the West Wing.) There were several ways to get White House–branded or presidentially branded "swag" around the campus. The president had several neat items that were available only if you asked the right people (usually the body guys—young assistants to the president who worked in the Oval Office), or if you were a visitor to the Oval Office. Those were usually the nicer cufflinks, American flag pins with the presidential seal on them, challenge coins, or even the "key to the White House," which was a beautiful gold key in an engraved wooden box. It's like a key to the city that a mayor gives to a hometown hero as an award for an extraordinary accomplishment, except it's from the president. During COVID times, visitors also could ask the body guys for cool-looking face masks with the presidential seal. The first lady had her own line of gifts as well (necklaces, earrings, trinket boxes, and so on).

At the gift shop, the visiting public could buy everyday office and home items as well as clothing. If you ever see a baby wearing a "Future President" onesie with a cute embroidered White House on it, chances are that it came from the White House Gift Shop in the EEOB. There is also a gift shop not on the White House campus across from the Treasury Department. That's where you go to get your cornier gifts, like a jacket with a giant seal of the president on it, and the seal has the wrong font and too many stars on it. That kind of stuff wasn't sold on the actual White House campus.

The gift shop had a rotating supply of coffee mugs that would change literally weekly. So one of our pastimes after getting coffee was running by the gift shop to see what had changed. Usually it was the mugs, and sometimes the shop would have new cufflinks and pins. The special items were the ones that had the president's signature engraved on them, or were branded "45." Those were collector's items. As staffers, we wanted to get those things *fast* and stock up for our friends and family. I shamelessly bought so many items from the gift shop that I'm pretty sure I bought every type of item you could get. And every White House staffer knew that it was the best place for birthday and Christmas shopping for as long as we worked there.

On my last day at the White House, folks were given parting gifts for their service. Luckily, I was offboarded a week before most and was able to grab the coolest swag bag before the good stuff ran out. It had a beautiful necklace and earrings set with the seal of the United States from the first lady's office, a commemorative pen and pad, and a "key to the White House." That was a rare gift. It's something I will always treasure and will display in my house for years to come.

Peanut Butter Cake, BY TERESA

Since this story is about gifts, it's only fitting that we pair it with a recipe for a birthday celebration! During the pandemic, nearly everyone had to celebrate their birthday at home. I wanted to make Brian's birthday very special by showing off my new pandemic baking skills. This peanut butter cake is the perfect dessert for a birthday celebration at home (and Brian's mom swears it has no calories!).

SERVES 8

1 box of chocolate cake mix, baked according to instructions
1 lb. (4 sticks) butter, softened
8 cups powdered sugar, divided
1¼ cup creamy peanut butter
7 Tbsp. whole milk, divided
¾ cup heavy cream
1½ cup semisweet chocolate chips
Pinch of salt
Peanut butter cup candies, chopped, divided

Bake the chocolate cake mix in two 9-inch cake pans and let cool.

Beat the butter until smooth. Add about half the sugar and beat again until smooth. Then add in the peanut butter and about half of the milk. Beat all the ingredients well, adding in the salt and remaining sugar. Add the remaining milk as needed until the frosting is thin enough to spread (but not too thin).

Heat the heavy cream in a pot until it begins to bubble, then pour in the chocolate chips. Let the mixture cook for about 2 minutes, then mix until smooth.

Top one cake layer with a coating of frosting, add a layer of chopped peanut butter cups, then add another layer of frosting. Add the second cake on top of that.

Frost the top and sides of the cake with the remaining frosting. Drizzle the chocolate-cream mixture all over the cake. Sprinkle with the remaining chopped peanut butter cups and then add birthday candles!

Ginger Old Fashioned, BY BRIAN

With something so sweet and delicious, you need a little spice. That's where the Ginger Old Fashioned comes into play. The Old Fashioned is a classic. Teresa's sister, Rosalia, added her own dash of flavor and kick to it—a healthy splash of ginger beer—and it is delicious. I am partial to Michter's rye for my Old Fashioneds, because I have a long-standing relationship with the brand's owners, the incomparable Magliocco brothers from New York, having represented them as their attorney for years, and because it is spectacular whiskey.

> 1 sugar cube or 1 tsp. simple syrup
> 2 oz. bourbon or rye whiskey (recommend Michter's)
> 2 dashes of Angostura bitters
> 1 healthy splash of ginger beer
> 1 maraschino cherry (or amaretto cherry for a little variety)
> 1 twist orange zest

Put a large ice cube or a few small ice cubes in a glass with the sugar cube or simple syrup. Pour in the whiskey, bitters, and ginger beer. Stir for about 15 seconds. Drop in the cherry. Twist the orange zest over the glass, drop it in, and serve.

CHAPTER 10

We Fell in Love to Zac Brown Band, Then Told Zac Brown About It

BY BRIAN

Teresa and I met for the first time at a birthday party in 2018 for our great mutual friends Morgan Ortagus, who would soon become the State Department spokesperson, and Katie Pavlich, a Fox News contributor and the editor of Townhall.com.

The fact that Teresa and I met at all is nothing short of a miracle.

First, we never would have met if President Trump had not won the 2016 election. Teresa was working on Capitol Hill for Congressman Tom Cole. I was an attorney at a large law firm in New York City. While we were staunch Republicans hoping against hope for Trump to beat Hillary Clinton, we both believed the estimates by the *New York Times*—or, as Trump referred to it, the "failing" *New York Times*—and others that Clinton had a 95 percent chance of winning the election. In other words, it seemed pretty much like a lost cause.

When Trump won, we were surprised, and ecstatic, and we both pursued positions in the administration, which were highly competitive. With some help from good friends and some luck, I ultimately secured a job as a senior advisor and speechwriter for Treasury Secretary Steven Mnuchin. Teresa was hired at the State Department to be special assistant to Assistant Secretary Marie Royce, and would have duties including writing and curating content for speeches.

On July 10, 2018, Teresa was feeling antisocial, as it was a Tuesday night and she was a bit melancholy after ending a long-term relationship in the months before. I was at work, also feeling antisocial, because I had a virtually unlimited amount of work to do and felt like a fish out of water in D.C., and because it was a Tuesday.

One of Teresa's friends did the old "Come onnnnnn, it'll be funnnnn" until she relented and agreed to go to the party. My friend and direct supervisor at the time, Assistant Secretary Tony Sayegh, similarly hit the right combination of optimism and peer pressure until I agreed. So we put our inhibitions and insecurities aside and went to the event, which was held at DBGB, a restaurant and bar owned by the famous chef Daniel Boulud.

When Tony and I arrived at the party, I spotted Teresa from across the room and blurted out to Tony, "Oh wow, she's cute." He replied, "Yeah, you should go talk to her," before placing his hand in my back and gently launching me in her direction, at which point I sort of ran/walked/stumbled up next to her, leaving me absolutely no choice but to say something. So I said, "Hi. I'm Brian." She smiled, laughed, and introduced herself. We went on to chat for a while and get to know each other. We found it interesting that we would both be tasked with speechwriting responsibilities, and agreed to continue the conversation over "professional drinks" to talk about…you know, uh, speechwriting—or something.

Our first date began as professional drinks but quickly devolved into something not at all professional. We began at a bar on Capitol Hill called Bourbon for a cocktail. We then decided to hop in an Uber to go sample the oyster shots at The Salt Line in Navy Yard. Later we attended

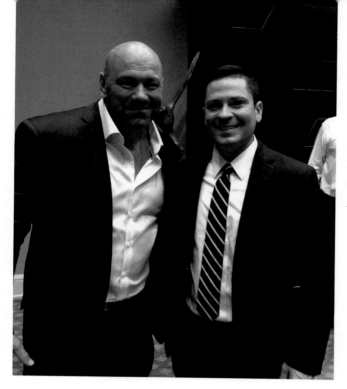

Brian with UFC President Dana White at the White House in August of 2020

Brian with Medal of Freedom recipient and Yankee legend Mariano Rivera in the White House press secretary's office on July 23, 2020

Brian and Teresa attend the swearing in of Justice Amy Coney Barrett in October 2020

Brian moderates a press conference with Treasury Secretary Steven Mnuchin at the spring meetings of the World Bank and IMF in April of 2019

Brian and Teresa take their first picture together at a Zac Brown Band concert on July 27, 2018

Photo by Kristen Garten Photography

Brian and Teresa get engaged on September 5, 2020

Brian and Teresa pose for a photo in the Oval Office in November of 2020

Brian and Teresa attend the signing of the National Defense Authorization Act on December 20, 2019

Brian and Teresa with legendary actor Jon Voight in front of the U.S. Capitol on August 14, 2020

Brian and Teresa pose for a photo at the Operation Warp Speed Vaccine Summit on December 8, 2020

*Brian and Teresa
with Kid Rock at
the White House
in December of
2020*

*Brian and Teresa
with their golden
retriever,
Larry Kudlow
Morgenstern*

Brian and Teresa meet Zac Brown in the Roosevelt Room of the White House in December of 2020

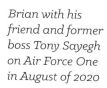

Brian with his friend and former boss Tony Sayegh on Air Force One in August of 2020

Brian meets with President Trump and senior staff to prepare for a press conference in Bedminster, New Jersey, in August of 2020

Brian attends a rally with President Trump in October of 2020

Brian in the Oval Office with President Trump, Press Secretary Kayleigh McEnany, and journalist Byron York on August 26, 2020

Brian in the Oval Office with President Trump, HHS Secretary Alex Azar, Senior Advisor Brad Smith, and OMB Director Russell Vought in November of 2020

Brian with Medal of Honor recipient Woody Williams in the West Wing lobby of the White House on September 2, 2020

Brian does a TV interview from the North Lawn of the White House

President Trump and Dave Portnoy share a laugh when Portnoy calls his dad from the patio outside the Oval Office on July 23, 2020

Brian and the White House Communications team take a photo with the president in January 2021

The White House Press team poses for a photo in Kayleigh McEnany's office in December of 2020

President Trump records a video message from the Resolute Desk in the Oval Office in November 2020

Teresa and friends watch President Trump leave the White House on Marine One in September 2020

Teresa poses for a photo at the Pentagon in September of 2020

Teresa and friends pose for a selfie in a mirror in the West Wing on Election Night 2020

Teresa poses with her colleagues Michael Bars and Ninio Fetalvo on the South Lawn in October of 2020

Teresa attends an Operation Warp Speed Event in the Rose Garden in September of 2020

Brian walks along the colonnade in the White House Rose Garden with President Trump on September 18, 2020

the opening night of a Mexican bar and restaurant called Mission, right across from Nationals Park, and owned by our mutual friend Fritz Brogan. In all, I believe we had bourbon, vodka, margaritas and, at some point, pizza—the latter while standing on the sidewalk.

Whatever it was—professional drinks or otherwise—it certainly went well enough to aim for a second date. I did so when I realized that Zac Brown Band would be playing at Nationals Park, practically next door to my apartment at the time. Teresa had spent most of her childhood in Georgia, and ZBB was a Georgia staple. They also happened to play some of the most fun, patriotic country music you'd ever heard.

So I invited Teresa to go, along with a couple of my friends and one of hers. We had drinks and food on the roof of my building overlooking the stadium before going to the concert, which was incredible. In addition to their own music, ZBB played a cover of Metallica's "Enter Sandman" that was one of the best performances I've ever witnessed. This had special meaning to me as a Mariano Rivera fan, because that song was played at Yankee Stadium whenever he entered a game.

Teresa and I took our first photo together at that concert. It is a blurry selfie taken in the dark, in the middle of a concert, surrounded by too many people. But it's one of my favorite pictures ever taken.

Over the ensuing years, Teresa and I dated and went through a lot together. During the coronavirus pandemic, we practically started living together, and we spent more time with each other than with anyone else.

As everyone knows, the country essentially had shut down. People all over the nation and world began working from home in close quarters with their significant others far more frequently than ever before, if they were able to keep their jobs at all. I have heard anecdotally that many relationships were accelerated in one direction or another. If fundamental problems existed, they were exposed quickly and profoundly, and relationships ended. On the other hand, if people were the right fit, they grew closer and their relationships became stronger faster than they otherwise would have. Thank God, Teresa and I were in the latter category.

In the late summer of 2020, I had been trying to come up with some-thing—anything—special and interesting for us to do together, since we and everyone else had been cooped up for too long. A couple of weeks before, Teresa and I had enjoyed a fantastic afternoon and evening with the legendary actor Jon Voight filming tribute videos for World War II veterans. As discussed in chapter six, Teresa and I shared the story with Jon of how we had met and fallen in love, and he believed in us so much that he actually suggested we elope at the Boar's Head Resort in Virginia. (We are spontaneous people, but we are not quite that spontaneous.)

It did get me thinking, though. I found a historic resort about three and a half hours from Washington in Hot Springs, Virginia, called the Omni Homestead. It was founded in the 1760s, and about half of America's presidents have stayed overnight there, including Thomas Jefferson, who visited the hot springs for their healing powers. It was the perfect place for patriotic history nerds like us to visit—doubly perfect because, well, it was open and functioning at a time when many places were closed for business because of the pandemic.

So, I whisked Teresa away for a long weekend trip, with the excuse to celebrate her birthday. The first stop at the Homestead was the shoot-ing club, which is at the top of a mountain on the resort grounds a short shuttle drive from the hotel. I had scheduled a lesson for us, so Teresa could learn how to properly shoot a shotgun. The lesson went well, in spite of the fact that my hands were sweating profusely—and despite my insisting on having my bulky backpack essentially glued to me the entire time.

After our lesson ended, we went inside the clubhouse at the shoot-ing range to pay the bill. The kind woman at the desk said, "Ya know, out back is a beautiful veranda where you can take some photos overlooking the mountain. You should do that before you head down." We looked at each other and said, "Okay, great!"

So out on the veranda we went. Teresa walked around marveling at how far we could see and how beautiful the view was.

I, on the other hand, was freaking out. You see, I had a surprise planned. It involved a photographer, who had instructed me to make our way to a piece of tape she would place on the ground, where she could take the perfect photo. There was no tape.

I spun around and looked back towards the building and saw a woman wearing a large hat lurking at the bottom of one of the windows. She was pointing at me and motioning with her fingers for me to grab Teresa and move her to the side.

So I walked up next to Teresa while she was looking out at the mountain, and I faced the woman in the hat, who, unbeknownst to Teresa, was behind her looking at us through a window about 25 feet away. The hat lady frantically pointed to my right, and I nodded. Then, without explanation, I put my hands on Teresa's shoulders and moved her to the right until the hat lady put her hand up as if to say "stop." Then I turned Teresa to face me. She was confused, to say the least, and I'm sure she was wondering why I was manhandling her like a weirdo. I looked back at the hat lady, and she gave me the "okay" sign to let me know we were in the right spot.

Then I looked into Teresa's eyes and started saying very romantic things. You see, when we'd entered the veranda, I had reached my sweaty paw into my conspicuous bag and pulled out a diamond ring, keeping it hidden from Teresa. At this moment, I got down on one knee and proposed to her (and she said yes!).

The hat lady—Kristen Garten, the wonderful photographer I had hired—leaped like a leopard out of nowhere, undetected, and started taking beautiful photos of us. Tanya, the gracious and helpful hotel staff member who had helped me plan the proposal, popped out of the club-house with flowers and Champagne. Our shooting instructor presented us with a souvenir clay target to commemorate the occasion.

It was a special moment. We drank Champagne and FaceTimed our families, and proceeded to have a spectacular, romantic weekend.

Fast-forward to December 2020, in the last month or so of the Trump administration. My office was in the West Wing across the hall from the Roosevelt Room, a popular holding area for visiting guests. I heard some people chatting across the hall, and I popped my head in to see who was there. It was none other than Zac Brown himself.

I had the great honor of meeting many interesting people at the White House—from Medal of Honor recipients to national champions to Medal of Freedom honorees. This situation felt like divine inter-vention. So I called Teresa and told her she needed to get over to the Roosevelt Room as soon as possible, which she did. We walked in to-gether and promptly interrupted Zac and whomever he was speaking with at the time.

We told him our story of how we had gone to his concert on our second date, taken our first picture together there, and gone on to fall in love. Now we were both working at the White House and were engaged to be married. We told him that we genuinely could not believe that we were getting to meet him in person to thank him for bringing us together, and that we were getting to do so in the West Wing of the White House.

The funny part is that I genuinely think that Zac was even more excited than we were to share this moment. His face lit up, and he smiled as wide as could be. He was an international superstar, and he was asking *us* if we would take a picture with *him*. The three of us ex-changed a few stories and marveled over how special it was to meet. Zac told us to reach out to him if there was ever a show we wanted to attend in the future, and that he'd love to say hello to us again when he was back around our way. Then Zac was whisked away on his VIP tour to see the Oval Office.

Once again, this moment was pretty pretty pretty pretty pretty good.

Navy Mess Cheese Grits and Shrimp, BY TERESA AND BRIAN

A logical choice to pair with this story, in honor of Zac Brown's hit song "Chicken Fried," would be—obviously—fried chicken and an ice-cold beer. But one of the dishes that truly inspired this book is the cheese grits from the Navy Mess in the West Wing, right near where we had our inspirational interaction with Zac. And there's hardly anything more Southern, or even more American, than shrimp and grits. Teresa ordered the grits every time the Navy Mess whipped them up. In fact, she would eat this dish as a whole meal—it was that good. We never got ahold of that actual recipe, but we've done our best to honor it with this creation.

SERVES 4

2 cups water, salted
3 Tbsp. chicken stock
½ cup boxed grits, uncooked
4 Tbsp. (½ stick) butter, divided
½ cup Parmesan
¼ cup Italian cheese mix
¼ cup cheddar
¼ cup ricotta (whole milk)
Salt and pepper to taste
2 cloves garlic, minced
1½ Tbsp. harissa seasoning
1 lb. shrimp, peeled and de-veined
Fresh parsley or oregano (optional, for garnish)

In a pot, bring the salted water and chicken stock to a boil. Once boiling, add in the grits and bring to a rolling boil. Lower the heat and simmer for about 10 minutes until the grits thicken. Still over low heat, add 2 Tbsp. of butter, ricotta, the other cheeses, chicken stock, and salt and pepper to taste, and whisk until blended.

In a nonstick pan, melt the other 2 Tbsp. butter with the garlic and harissa seasoning, and sauté the shrimp for about 2 minutes on each side until warm and pink. Serve the grits with the shrimp artfully arranged on top. Garnish with some fresh parsley or oregano to make the dish really sing.

TO DRINK

Emaciated Margarita, BY BRIAN

Cheese grits are rich, so they pair well with a light, crisp beverage that's not too sweet. "Skinny" margaritas, which have fewer calories than the traditional ones, are all the rage these days. But why would you drink a skinny margarita when you can drink an emaciated one? If you enjoy tequila and don't want something with too much sugar, then this drink is for you.

    2 oz. silver tequila
    4 oz. club soda
    1 tsp. simple syrup or 1 packet of sweetener
    1 generous squirt of lime juice
    1 slice orange or lime

Put some ice cubes in a shaker. Pour the tequila, club soda, simple syrup or sweetener, and lime juice over the ice. Shake well. Pour into a glass and garnish with the orange or lime slice.

CHAPTER 11

The Night RBG Passed Away

BY BRIAN

On September 18, 2020, I boarded Air Force One to accompany President Trump on a trip to a rally in Bemidji, Minnesota. If you have never heard of Bemidji, Minnesota, I assure you, you are not alone. If you live in Bemidji, you might be alone, because you might be the only person who lives there. The point is, it's a very small town. On this particular evening, tens of thousands of people were in Bemidji to see President Trump.

The thing a lot of my friends from blue states don't understand is that Trump rallies are unlike anything they have ever been to, except maybe a WWE event. The crowd is rowdy. The crowd cheers and laughs when Trump cracks a joke. The crowd boos when he mentions Democrats or RINOs (Republicans in name only). They really are love fests, as Trump describes them.

On the way to this particular love fest, I spoke with President Trump in his cabin on the plane regarding the draft of his speech. He told me to make sure it had lines about how the Obama administration had killed the iron ore industry (pronounced "in-DUS-tree") in Minnesota and how

Trump had brought it back. The president also told me to summon Stephen Miller, his chief speechwriter, to his cabin and to let "Steve" know that the speech was "boring."

Evidently, Trump wasn't satisfied with the speech as written, because with the exception of a few acknowledgments of the VIPs in the crowd, he never read a word of it onstage. He riffed. He riffed about "Sleepy Joe." He riffed about Speaker of the House Nancy Pelosi and the Democrats. He riffed about tax cuts. He riffed about "ridiculous, endless wars." He covered all the greatest hits. He riffed for a solid two-plus hours without missing a beat. Toward the end of the speech, someone (I can't for the life of me remember who) walked past the teleprompter operator and asked, "Where is he in the speech?" The response was, "He hasn't touched it."

While President Trump was enjoying his rapport with the crowd, and they were enjoying their time with him, he was not aware of what had happened shortly after he took the stage. One of the most iconic Americans in our nation's history, Justice Ruth Bader Ginsburg, had passed away.

We staff members traveling with the president that night huddled up out of sight of the press corps to address the obvious question: What should we do?

Should one of us walk up onstage and pass him a note? Should we put a message for him in the teleprompter? Should we choose not to disrupt the event and tell him what happened after he finished speaking?

In thinking through our options, we honestly were concerned about what might happen if we interrupted his speech. Justice Ginsburg was, famously, not a fan of President Trump. And the president was on a roll. The laughter and boos were constantly ebbing and flowing. If we interrupted him and the first words out of his mouth were "Ruth Bader Ginsburg," there was a chance that some people in the audience who did not know what had happened would start booing. Obviously, we could not have such a thing happen. This was a time for mourning and respect no matter what.

So we got to work on a statement honoring Justice Ginsburg's life and contributions to the country, and her family and colleagues.

Thanks to White House counselor Hope Hicks, I have a copy of one of the drafts we worked on signed by President Trump to mark the historic occasion. It feels strange to have a keepsake from the event of someone's death. I mean no disrespect to the Ginsburg family. In fact, Justice Ginsburg's daughter was a professor of mine in law school, and I quite liked her. I just cannot imagine ever again finding myself on Air Force One with the president of the United States when an iconic Supreme Court justice dies. So I still have the signed draft.

Following the president's speech, as he began to walk off the stage, I went up ahead to board the plane from the staff entrance in the back. The plan was for Dan Scavino to walk with the president and tell him to go straight up the stairs onto the plane and into his cabin. You see, sometimes President Trump would stop at the bottom of the stairs before boarding the plane and gaggle with the press corps. We were trying to avoid that happening this time, because we wanted to let him know about Justice Ginsburg privately and give him time to review and edit our draft statement.

As I walked up the stairs, it was difficult to see in detail what was happening as the president made his way from the podium, waved to supporters, clapped, and gave his trademark thumbs-up. From the vantage point of people near the plane, including myself and the press corps, the lights near the stage were extremely bright and the music was extremely loud.

I continued up the stairs and onto the plane. Then something clicked in my head. What if Dan didn't get a chance to tell the president to go straight onto the plane? What if they couldn't hear each other? What if the crowd, the lights, the blaring music, or the sound of the plane engine got in the way? What if, for whatever reason, Trump stopped in front of the press corps before he boarded? I had to get off the plane.

I ran back down the rear stairs and over to the press corps assembled in their customary spot: beneath the wing near the bottom of the stairs that the president used to board the plane.

President Trump walked towards us, still making no indication as to whether he would head straight up the stairs or stop at the bottom. As he got closer, my heart raced. Then he stopped. He looked in our direction. It was a surreal moment. Elton John's "Tiny Dancer" was playing from the speakers around the stage he had left behind.

A female reporter yelled to him. It was difficult to hear what she said exactly over all the noise and because the reporter was wearing a mask, but it was just clear enough to make out the words about Ginsburg's death. Surprised, Trump responded: "She just died? Wow. I didn't know that. I just, ah, you're telling me now for the first time." He paused, looked down, and spread his hands apart in one of his famous expressive ways, then looked back up. "She led an amazing life," the president said. "What else can you say? She was an amazing woman. Whether you agreed or not, she was an amazing woman who led an amazing life. I'm actually saddened to hear that. I am saddened to hear that. Thank you very much." The video is now very famous, and if you haven't watched it, please do.

I try to look at funerals, memorials, and the like as celebrations of life. I realize that is not everyone's view, and it can be exceedingly difficult to have this outlook in the face of profound sadness. But I have to believe that if one of my family members passed away, and he or she received a moment of commemoration like that from the president of the United States, it would lend a certain degree of comfort and pride that my relative had had a life well-lived.

Mom's Beef Stroganoff, BY BRIAN

When unexpected events occur, I turn to comfort food. Nothing quite fits that mold better than my mom's beef stroganoff, which she so kindly and generously has allowed me to publish the recipe for here. It was fun to put it together, because she usually just makes this using her instincts rather than a recipe.

MAKES 6 GENEROUS SERVINGS

8 oz. mushrooms, wiped and thinly sliced
12 Tbsp. butter, divided
Frozen peas (optional)
4 Tbsp. olive oil, divided
1 onion, chopped
3 cups flour, divided
Salt and pepper to taste
2 lbs. beef round cubes
2 cups beef broth
1 cup red wine
½ cup sour cream
1 (12- to 16-oz.) bag egg noodles
Fresh parsley, for garnish

Use a wet paper towel to wipe down the mushrooms. Slice them thinly. In a pan, melt 3 Tbsp. butter, put in the mushrooms, and sauté them on low heat until soft. (Add some frozen peas if desired.) In a separate pan, heat 2 Tbsp. each of oil and butter. Put in the chopped onion and sauté until they're soft and a light golden color.

(continued)

Put 2 cups flour in a dish and add salt and pepper. Dredge the beef cubes in the mixture. In a deep pan, heat 2 Tbsp. olive oil and brown the beef cubes in the oil.

In a separate pot, melt 6 Tbsp. butter. Add 6 Tbsp. flour and stir into a paste. Slowly add the beef broth and red wine. Stir over low heat until thickened into gravy.

Pour the gravy over the meat in the pan. Add the mushrooms and onions. Simmer over low heat for 20 minutes, stirring occasionally to keep the gravy from sticking. Add the sour cream and stir until heated through.

While the beef is simmering, boil the egg noodles in salted water until they are al dente, and drain. Stir in 1 Tbsp. butter to keep the noodles from sticking.

On serving plates, create an even bed of the noodles and spoon the beef stroganoff over the noodles. Season to taste with salt and pepper, and garnish with fresh parsley.

Tip: For a short cut, instead of using beef broth and the onion mixture, just use 2 cups canned French onion soup.

Red Wine with Dinner; Lemon Meringue Martini for Dessert, BY BRIAN

Nothing pairs better with a rich dish like this than a smooth red wine, like the merlot from Josh Cellars, which I think is quite good and modestly priced.

After dinner, you'll probably want something sweet and strong to continue the path to comfort. This dessert drink also comes courtesy of my mom.

Lemon Meringue Martini

2 oz. light rum
1 oz. limoncello crema
1 oz. Grand Marnier
Sugar and lemon or lime wedge, for garnish

Fill a shaker with crushed ice. Pour in the ingredients. Shake very well for about 30 seconds, until the drink is thoroughly mixed and chilled. Cut a lemon or lime wedge down the middle so it will sit on the edge of the glass. Rub the fruit around the rim, and dip the rim in sugar. Strain the drink into the glass.

CHAPTER 12

ACB's Swearing In

BY TERESA

In the lead-up to the 2020 presidential election, President Trump had the opportunity to nominate a Supreme Court justice after the death of Ruth Bader Ginsberg. Viewing this sad and historic occasion through a political lens, it was a winning issue for the president. He had the chance to add another conservative justice, something he had already done twice during his presidency.

Trump nominated Amy Coney Barrett, a woman, a Catholic, and a judge with a strong record of hundreds of well-reasoned opinions. Brian, being the legal scholar he is, could not have been more excited to be a part of the process and team to confirm a Supreme Court justice, something that does not happen very often.

Amy Coney Barrett's confirmation proceeding spoke for itself—or, rather, she certainly spoke for herself. She impressed not only particular members of the Senate Judiciary Committee but public officials on both sides of the aisle, the media, and pretty much all of America. She is an incredible role model for women and girls in this country. She was confirmed with flying colors.

Brian was there in the Rose Garden when Trump announced that Barrett would be the nominee. And we were both given the chance to witness her swearing in, which happened very quickly after her Senate confirmation.

When the White House hosts an event where the president is speaking, very senior staff are usually the only people formally invited to attend. But there are many chances for those in and around the complex to join as well.

It was incredible what the operations staff pulled together in such a short amount of time after Barrett was confirmed. Staged on the South Lawn, her swearing in was one of the most impressive setups I've ever seen at the White House. Several American flags hung boldly between the columns of the south side of the White House (where the residential balcony, known as the Truman Balcony, is). Lights illuminated the South Portico, and the Marine Band played beautiful music.

It was after sundown and dark. Brian and I originally stood in the back with the press and some fellow staff members, but quickly realized that we could probably move up to the seating and fill some chairs; the ceremony would begin shortly. To our pleasant surprise, a couple of chairs were available near the front. Suddenly, we found ourselves sitting next to members of Congress, cabinet secretaries, and other VIPs. Even better, we had a fantastic view of the podium.

The swearing in was historic and an honor to witness. President Trump and Barrett both spoke eloquently, and Justice Clarence Thomas administered the oath of office in a deep, clear, and booming voice. After the brief but poignant ceremony concluded, we proceeded to leave our seats and head toward the exit. As we did so, we decided to grab a few more photos in front of the South Portico and the draped flags. Without having someone nearby to take our photo, we opted for selfies.

It wasn't too long before I heard someone say, "Do you want me to take your photo?" I turned around and saw that a VIP cabinet secretary had approached us. It wasn't just any cabinet secretary; it was Elaine Chao, who had served as the secretary of labor during George W. Bush's presidency and was now serving as the secretary of transportation under President Trump. She also happened to be Senator Mitch McConnell's wife. I had always admired her. She was the first Asian American to hold several high-level positions in government and was the matriarch of the conservative Asian American community. As someone who was beginning to reconnect to my heritage and culture with my mother, as well as engage with conservatives in the Asian Pacific Islander space, I truly admired and respected her. And on a funny note, she also looks strikingly like my mother (who has been mistaken for her—it must be the hair).

We of course accepted her offer to take our photo. When she finished, she approached me and bluntly asked, "Who are you, and why don't I know you?" I was slightly shocked at first, but then realized that Elaine Chao truly was passionate about caring for those in the conservative Asian American community. The pageant girl in me is trained to respond on the spot, so I just rattled off my entire résumé and introduced her properly to Brian. And then without hesitation, I stupidly blurted out, "You and my mother look just alike!" I felt silly for doing that, but I had my chance and just wanted to say it. She seemed flattered, but I quickly thanked her and walked away, embarrassed.

After that night, she was gracious enough to speak with me at length privately and give me career advice. In fact, I have come to learn that she frequently provides an ear and support to many young people trying to make their way in the world of politics. Politics is a nasty business, and so it has been heartening for me to learn that someone as powerful as Elaine Chao can still be kind and generous, and for that, she has my deep respect.

After our interaction with Secretary Chao, Brian went back into the West Wing because he had one more thing he wanted to do before we went home. He had been an enthusiastic supporter of Barrett's nomination and had defended her in the media throughout the process. And so he grabbed a souvenir copy of the Constitution, which he had been keeping in his desk, and went up the stairs to the White House counsel's suite, where the new justice and her family were gathered. He approached "ACB," as she had become known, and said, "Justice Barrett, I wanted to congratulate you and ask if you'd sign my Constitution for me." She responded, a little surprised, and said, "I think you're the first person to call me Justice Barrett." She was flattered and signed the document with perfect penmanship. Brian congratulated her again, as well as members of the confirmation team and the White House counsel's office, and finally, we went home for the night.

Mom's Blueberry Cream Cheesecake, BY TERESA

Since this story involved my mom's famous lookalike, it's only fitting to include one of my mom's great recipes, and this dessert is a real crowd pleaser! Growing up, I always loved it when my mother made this dessert, because it meant I could lick the delicious icing off the bowl when she was finished. The icing is the star of this dish. I'd say it's the perfect Fourth of July picnic dish, but really it can be served year-round.

SERVES 10

½ cup (1 stick) butter
¼ cup (half a stick) margarine
⅓ cup brown sugar
Half an egg, slightly beaten
1½ cups pecans or walnuts, chopped
12 oz. cream cheese
½ cup sugar
⅓ cup milk
8 oz. Cool Whip
1 can blueberry pie filling
Fresh blueberries (optional)

Preheat the oven to 350°F. In a bowl, mix the butter, margarine, brown sugar, egg, and nuts. Once mixed well, spread into a 9-by-12-inch buttered baking dish. Bake in the oven for 25 minutes.

While the crust is cooking, create the icing by blending the cream cheese, sugar, and milk in a bowl with a hand mixer. Add the Cool Whip to the icing when it's creamy.

Remove the crust from the oven and let it cool. Once cooled, spread the icing over the crust. Then spread the blueberry filling over that. Serve and store the remainder in the refrigerator.

Tip: Add fresh blueberries to the pie filling for a special touch.

TO DRINK

Irish Coffee, BY BRIAN

Since the cheesecake is great for either a sweet breakfast or a delicious dessert, it makes sense to pair it with a coffee drink. The Irish coffee can be served hot or poured over ice.

- 6 oz. brewed coffee
- 1 Tbsp. sugar or sweetener
- 2 oz. whiskey (typically Jameson)
- 1½ oz. Irish cream (typically Bailey's, but there are other good ones out there)

Pour the coffee into a glass, keeping it hot or pouring it over ice. Add the sugar or sweetener and whiskey. Stir. Pour the Irish cream on top in a circular motion and let it swirl in.

CHAPTER 13

Coronavirus Task Force Battles

BY BRIAN

Assembling a government task force nearly always involves turf wars between bureaucratic teams wanting supremacy. The coronavirus task force was no different.

Dr. Deborah Birx was an ambassador during the George W. Bush Administration known for her work in Africa on the President's Emergency Plan for AIDS Relief (PEPFAR), and was awarded continued service in global health positions during the Obama administration and the early years of the Trump administration. When President Trump established the Coronavirus Task Force, he named Dr. Birx as the coordinator.

Dr. Birx certainly erred on the side of caution when it came to coronavirus restrictions, and that is putting it very mildly. She and Fauci were principal proponents of lockdowns, and she often justified her decisions based on the number of multigenerational families in America. Her classic, hypothetical fact pattern she used to justify her recommendations was young people leaving the house, becoming exposed to the virus, then returning home and hugging their grandmothers, giving them COVID, and killing them.

Dr. Scott Atlas was a fellow at the Hoover Institution at Stanford and a public health policy expert hired by President Trump to join the task force. He pointed out that these facts simply do not apply to everyone. Dr. Atlas represented a view on the task force that was contrary to several of the doctors because he advocated for policies that bore in mind more than just coronavirus risk.

Atlas advocated for intense protection of the elderly and otherwise vulnerable, but a return to relative normalcy for the majority of the population. He cited data regarding the population at risk of dying from coronavirus, which was overwhelmingly elderly Americans and those with existing comorbidities; along with data regarding the health effects of missed checkups, surgeries, and other medical appointments; as well as data regarding depression and substance abuse due to reduced socialization. Paraphrasing a favorite comment of President Trump, Dr. Atlas was the voice in the room stating that the cure cannot be worse than the disease.

Dr. Birx did not appreciate Dr. Atlas' challenges to her recommendations and would let anyone who would listen know about it. She said, on more than one occasion, that Atlas was "literally killing people." She came under fire herself after advocating for strict compliance with lockdowns when the Associated Press ran a story chronicling her own multigenerational family gathering at holidays, and her need to personally attend to elderly relatives despite working in environments where she could have been exposed to the virus.

Dr. Robert Redfield was the director of the CDC during the Trump administration. He was tasked with running an agency run amok, but in turn the agency seemed to run him. In late September 2020, he arrived at one task force meeting hat in hand asking for approval of a plan to ban the cruise industry from operating for six months—a so-called "no sail" order. His request was roundly rejected, and for good reason. He only meekly presented the proposal, and it was clear that the career leadership at the agency had bullied him into advocating for it.

Vice President Mike Pence, who chaired the task force, responded graciously, but firmly, on behalf of everyone else in the room. He stated that a no sail order was in place, and that it could be renewed—or not—every thirty days. He also pointed out that the cruise industry employed about seven hundred thousand people, and so we should be working with the industry to find a way to reopen safely, not ban it from functioning for arbitrary lengths of time.

Of course, the story leaked immediately to the media that the CDC was subjected to undue political influence and that the Trump administration refused to "follow the science." This was a routine occurrence. Senior administration officials were regularly attacked by nameless and faceless bureaucrats at the CDC, who often wanted power to make decisions that were above their paygrades. They also frequently complained that they did not get to do their own press conferences often enough. They thought that their turf was being encroached upon, and they acted out.

The fact is that the CDC officials needed the supervision they were receiving because they had made so many mistakes. Over the course of the pandemic, CDC staff had sent flawed COVID-19 tests to states, posted mistaken draft guidance pertaining to how the virus spreads, tried to stop people from singing in church, made changes to testing and social distancing recommendations without appropriate coordination with other agencies or states, and recommended canceling trick-or-treating on Halloween (an activity that takes place outdoors with children, who were the lowest risk population), among other blunders.

Dr. Redfield also reacted poorly to Dr. Atlas' challenges to policy recommendations. Redfield was overheard by an NBC reporter on a commercial airplane complaining about Dr. Atlas to someone on the other end of a cell phone conversation.

All of the little battles seemed to pale in comparison to one, though, which was when Dr. Birx stated in a task force meeting, sitting right next to Vice President Pence, that the administration was not taking the coronavirus seriously.

You could hear a pin drop. It was an outrageous comment, and the vice president didn't take kindly to it. President Trump had established the task force and appointed the vice president to chair it. The president had shut down travel from China and Europe. He had established Operation Warp Speed to develop vaccines and therapeutics in record time. He had overseen—at Birx' recommendation—a total shutdown of the economy. He signed numerous pieces of legislation providing public health and economic relief totaling trillions of dollars. The notion that the administration wasn't taking it seriously was simply preposterous and insulting, and it parroted the false talking points of the Biden campaign during the election season.

The vice president responded in a way that was as animated as I ever saw him. He was always a calm person. That day, he said sternly, "Deb, over these months, I like to think that we've become great friends. But I am not going to sit here and let you say that this administration isn't taking this seriously." He went on to commend the service of the professionals on the task force—dozens of them around the room—and pointed out how everyone had been working day and night to help the country weather the crisis.

The coronavirus task force was an intense place. The pressure on the medical professionals in that room was palpable. The competition was fierce. I like to believe that everyone there was advocating for policies based on their best judgment. But at the same time, it is undeniable that they are human beings with egos, and they had bureaucratic turf to protect. With the doctors, it wasn't always about "the science." Sometimes it was about the politics.

Arugula Salad with Turf War Dressing, BY TERESA

It makes sense to pair a chapter about the doctors with a light and healthy salad—topped with a complex dressing. In this recipe, the spicy and sweet flavors will compete for the diners' affections, resulting in a unique and delicious kick.

Salad

Desired amount of arugula
Marcona almonds (optional, for garnish)
Turf War Dressing (recipe below)

Spread the dressing over a bed of arugula and add Marcona almonds for garnish (and protein) if desired.

Turf War Dressing

MAKES ABOUT ¾ CUP

¼ cup mayonnaise
2 Tbsp. shallots, chopped
2 tsp. olive oil
1 Jalapeño pepper, chopped
1 clove garlic, chopped
2 Tbsp. cilantro, chopped
1 lime, juiced
¼ tsp. salt
¼ tsp. pepper
1 tsp. honey

Blend the ingredients together until smooth.

TO DRINK

No-Collusion Mule, BY BRIAN

Moscow Mules are delicious. Unfortunately, no one working in the Trump administration could mention anything remotely associated with Russia without some harebrained conspiracy theorist screaming, "Collusion!" So I renamed the Moscow Mule the No-Collusion Mule.

> 2 oz. vodka
> 1 tsp. lime juice
> 3 to 4 oz. ginger beer
> Slices of lime, for garnish

Fill a glass—or better, a copper mug—with crushed ice cubes. Pour in all the ingredients except the lime slice, stir, and serve with a lime slice on the edge of the glass.

CHAPTER 14

Election Night 2020

BY TERESA

The 2020 presidential election was one of the wildest elections in history. And being a staffer in the White House on Election Night during one of the wildest elections in history was pretty incredible. There was so much excitement in the air, tons of chatter, and plenty of nervous optimism. We all felt good about the president's performance during the campaign. Brian had traveled with him to some of the rallies, and the energy surely transmitted from those rallies to the staff in the hallways of the West Wing.

As official staff instead of campaign staff, we weren't allowed to do much on Election Day but watch the excitement fill the air. Reporters from news channels around the world arrived during the early morning to set up for live shots at Pebble Beach, the nickname for the gravel area right outside the doors of the West Wing. Supporters were walking around the streets of Washington with campaign gear. And eight-foot-tall fences loomed over the perimeter of the White House complex, as the Secret Service was anticipating a strong reaction from the public over the election results.

It was a beautiful day in Washington. The temperature wasn't too cold, the air was crisp, and there was not a cloud in the sky. I had become really close friends with my officemate, fellow communications staffer Ninio Fetalvo, during my time at the White House, and we had been preparing for Election Day for weeks—this was supposed to be a party! We created a Spotify playlist, made runs to the liquor store, planned a fancy lunch break at our favorite spot (Joe's Seafood in downtown D.C., just a couple of blocks away), and let all of our friends on staff know that they were welcome to visit our office, room 182 in the EEOB, to watch the polling coverage and the results roll in throughout the day.

By some divine intervention, on our walk to our "fancy" lunch we ran into a whole group of friends who were also headed to Joe's. But they had even "fancier" plans than we had—they had reserved a private room in the back. Now that's how you spend an Election Day lunch. We each splurged on a glass of wine, which we would not normally have had with lunch, and some really decadent dishes, including big plates of some of the most delicious and greasy fried chicken you could ever have. We enjoyed one another's company and just generally prepared ourselves for what we hoped would be a short and successful night.

Because of COVID, the D.C. government had placed strict limitations on the number of people allowed in venues around the city. But the D.C. government does not have jurisdiction in the White House, which is federal property. And so the Trump campaign had decided to have its headquarters at the White House, with a stage set up in the East Room of the mansion.

Around the close of business, Ninio and I decided to get the pregame festivities going in our office in the EEOB. After a little while, we walked next door to the West Wing to say hello to some friends who had come over to watch the returns. There were hundreds of staff members walking around the West Wing, hugging each other, laughing, and having a great time. I have so many great pictures and memories from that night.

Luckily, Brian had a prime office location in the West Wing. Granted, the West Wing is not that big, so his office was the size of a closet. But to have an office in the West Wing is a luxury and a big deal. So we went into his office to get away from the crowd for a minute, and to chat with friends who had stopped over from other agencies in the federal government. We ordered pizza and wings from the Navy Mess, and watched the commentary on the news. My heart was pounding over what was happening in Georgia, where I grew up. We couldn't believe that the state had so many issues counting votes.

Speaking of the Navy Mess, that is the White House dining room in the West Wing. Only certain staff members are allowed to eat there or order takeout from there. Those staff members are commissioned officers, known as special assistants, deputy assistants, and assistants to the president. In terms of diplomatic rank, they fall somewhere below cabinet secretaries but above most military generals. Since Brian had one of those commissions as a special assistant to the president (SAP), I helped myself to his Navy Mess account, which he paid for(!) and which the incredible staff there were happy to allow.

We ordered *a lot* of food from the Navy Mess that night. After dinnertime, it essentially serves only "bar food" for people working late, so the menu consisted of wings, pizza, and my favorite, mozzarella sticks. I don't know how the cooks there make mozzarella sticks special, but those things are so good that I wish I could have some right now. Anyway, around eight p.m., Ninio and I went down to the Mess to pick up our order. I tried to carry the stack of boxes full of delicious food gracefully through the crowd of people—after perhaps one too many cocktails.

It wasn't long before I turned a corner and *splat*. I had dropped my precious box of mozzarella sticks, and with that, a whole cup of red marinara sauce, on the beautiful carpet of the West Wing, right on the main thoroughfare. Ninio and I just stared at each other and could not believe it had happened. Just then, Kayleigh McEnany walked through, looked at each of us, and started laughing. Thank God she did. That made Ninio and me laugh too, and we felt so much better. She was really kind, asking if we needed a hand and helping us to get a grip when we were panicking. We went back over to the Mess and grabbed fistfuls of napkins.

I crawled on the floor in my cute red dress and started wiping the spill with the napkins. I was able to get some of it cleaned up, but there was no way to make it seem like it had never happened. I mean, this was a *spill*. Eventually, I gave up and placed an open napkin over the remaining red spot, hoping that I could flag down a member of the dedicated cleaning staff to do a more professional job. I took a lap around the hall but did not find anyone. A little while later, I walked down towards the Mess again and saw that it had all been cleaned up! Thank God, and thank whoever was able to do that. I think, I hope, that no one except Kayleigh, Ninio, and I ever knew that I was responsible for the Great Marinara Incident of 2020 on Election Night until now.

While all of this was going on, of course, there were tense and violent scuffles going on in the streets around the White House caused by left-wing Black Lives Matter and antifa thugs. With the help of the Secret Service agents who were securing the area, we were able to get home peacefully, and the marinara spill was the only messy thing that happened to us.

TO EAT

Dat's a Spicy Pizza, BY BRIAN

*I like my pizza thin, crispy, and spicy. You can use a store-bought pizza crust,
but I prefer to make my own using double-zero (00) flour.*

MAKES 2 PIZZAS; SERVES 4

¼ tsp. active dry yeast
½ tsp. granulated sugar
¼ cup warm water
½ cup cool water
2 cups 00 flour, divided
1 tsp. salt
2 Tbsp. extra-virgin olive oil
1 14-oz. jar or can pizza sauce
12 oz. shredded mozzarella
1 cup ricotta
3 oz. grated Parmesan
8 oz. pepperoni, sliced
6 oz. banana pepper rings
Oregano
Cracked red pepper

Dissolve the yeast and sugar in warm water, stirring. In a mixing bowl,
combine the dissolved mixture and the cool water. Begin mixing slowly.
While mixing, add in about a quarter of the flour. Continue mixing until
it becomes a smooth batter. Add the next quarter of flour and continue
mixing. Add the third and fourth quarters of the flour, and the salt, and
continue mixing. Once the dough is well mixed and smooth, let it rest for
5 to 10 minutes. Then knead the dough for about 7 to 10 minutes.

Form the dough into a ball. Lightly coat a bowl with extra-virgin olive oil. Put the dough into the bowl, cover it with plastic wrap, and let it sit for 1 to 2 hours.

Flour a baking pan or the countertop. Place the dough on the surface and punch to release the gas. Tear the dough in half so you can make two crusts. Roll out one of the pieces of dough until it forms a thin, circular 10- to 12-inch crust.

Preheat the oven to 450°F.

Spoon about a third to half of the pizza sauce generously on the crust and spread it around until there is a robust layer. Spread about half the shredded mozzarella across the crust to cover it with a thin layer. Strategically place small dollops of ricotta all over the crust. Place pepperoni slices and banana pepper rings between the dollops of ricotta. Generously season with oregano and cracked red pepper.

Place the pizza on a pizza board, or on tin foil on a baking sheet. Cook in the oven for about 10 minutes, until the crust looks golden and the cheese is bubbling. Then broil for 1 to 2 minutes to crisp everything.

Take the pizza out of the oven, sprinkle a light layer of Parmesan on top, and let it melt while sprinkling a bit more cracked red pepper on top. Let the pizza cool for at least 3 minutes before serving.

Citrus Sangria, BY BRIAN

Nothing pairs better with a spicy red dish than a light, sweet, bubbly beverage—like citrus sangria.

2 750-ml bottles dry rosé wine
1 lemon, sliced
1 lime, sliced
1 orange, sliced
4 oz. brandy
12 oz. pineapple juice
12 oz. soda water (seltzer)
Extra fruit, for garnish

In a large pitcher or punch bowl, mix all the ingredients, then chill in the refrigerator. Serve over ice with fruit garnish.

CHAPTER 15

Pfizer, the FDA, and the Biden Campaign Colluded to Rig the Election

BY BRIAN

In 2020, President Trump and his team launched Operation Warp Speed to create vaccines five times faster than ever before in an effort to bring the coronavirus pandemic to an end as soon as possible. The effort involved several vaccine companies, various agencies in the Department of Health and Human Services, the Department of Defense for logistical support, and members of the scientific community.

During the summer and early fall of 2020, Pfizer CEO Albert Bourla repeatedly stated that the company hoped to have its initial vaccine efficacy data available by October after its clinical trial hit thirty-two confirmed cases of the virus.[1] That means Pfizer potentially would be able to tell the public before Election Day on November 3, 2020, that thanks to Operation Warp Speed, its vaccine would work to combat the virus. Such an announcement could have given President Trump momentum and credit heading into the final weeks and days of the campaign.

The Democrats and their allies would not tolerate that. Even though such an announcement would have been positive, life-saving news for America and the world, winning the election was more important to them. So they promptly began a political campaign to prevent the announcement from happening, and to delay the approval process—potentially costing thousands of lives. Leading up to the election, career bureaucrats at the Food and Drug Administration and left-wing medical lobbyists affiliated with the Biden campaign colluded with Pfizer to change the plan that had been in place for months.

Let's review the timeline.

In June, the FDA issued guidance to vaccine manufacturers outlining what they would look for in clinical trials. It included the same six-week waiting period that other vaccine trials required, after the time a median patient in a trial had received their final vaccine dose, to ensure that adverse reactions were accounted for.[2]

Also in June, Dr. Ezekiel Emanuel published an op-ed in the *New York Times* alleging that an approved vaccine before the election would be a "campaign stunt" for President Trump and essentially argued that no trial results should be released before the election.[3] Emanuel was a health care advisor to the Biden campaign. He is also the brother of Rahm Emanuel, who was formerly White House chief of staff under Obama, and is the author of an infamous, vile, evil op-ed arguing that life is not worth living past the age of seventy-five.[4] It's worth noting that Joe Biden became president at age seventy-eight, with Emanuel's support.

In September, Albert Bourla stated that Pfizer anticipated seeing results of their vaccine trials by October—in other words, before the election.[5]

Also in September, both Joe Biden and Kamala Harris declared that they did not trust Donald Trump to deliver a safe vaccine.[6,7]

On October 1, 2020, Zeke Emanuel led a group of partisan so-called thought leaders to openly, publicly, aggressively—and successfully—lobby Pfizer and the FDA to delay announcing results until after the election.[8]

On October 6, 2020, the FDA altered its own guidance to change the standard six-week waiting period to a two-month waiting period.[9] Its preposterous justification was that an extra eighteen days added on to the waiting period would reduce overall vaccine hesitancy, hesitancy championed by Joe Biden and Kamala Harris.[10] The very idea is ridiculous—this notion that Americans who were vaccine hesitant would suddenly change their minds because of a slightly longer waiting period in an arcane approval process in a Washington, D.C. bureaucracy.

Shortly thereafter, Emanuel met privately with Pfizer's CEO and subsequently bragged about advising him on what to say publicly about delaying the results.[11]

Then, by mid-October, Pfizer stated publicly that there would be no results announced before the election.[12]

To be clear, Pfizer could have accessed information about its clinical trial following the original thirty-two-case threshold and informed the public of its success.[13] They chose not to, after their meeting with Emanuel and after the FDA inexplicably changed its rules, Pfizer later citing "discussions" with the FDA as justification.[14]

Also after meeting with Ezekiel Emanuel, a Pfizer executive made the preposterous claim that the company was not a part of Operation Warp Speed. These comments can only be described as splitting hairs, cynically and dishonestly, by stating that because they did not have a "research and development" contract, they were not a part of President Trump's successful program.[15]

Right. So, even though they were receiving *billions* of dollars from the program, and benefited from the revolutionary, fast-tracked regulatory process, Operation Warp Speed had nothing to do with their success? These people wanted to distance themselves from Trump so badly that they tried to convince the public that money is not, in fact, fungible. Good luck with that.

Also subsequent to meeting with Emanuel, someone leaked a story to the press stating that vaccine manufacturers had decided to snub the Trump White House when they were allegedly invited to participate in a vaccine summit to explain the vaccine development and distribution process and reduce vaccine hesitancy. It was fake news. They did not snub the White House. The FDA, which regulates the vaccine manufacturers, thought it best not to have them there while applications were potentially in process. I explained that to reporters. A manufacturer other than Pfizer corroborated the story. The press didn't care. They ran the story anyway.[16]

In any event, the data finally became available—magically—on Sunday, November 8, 2020. For anyone keeping score, that is one day after the mainstream media declared that Joe Biden had won the election.[17] It was literally the next day. They weren't even trying to hide the timing.

Pfizer CEO Albert Bourla also cashed in $5.6 million in stock on that very same day.[18] His team claimed it was a prescheduled event, and the two things had nothing to do with each other. If anyone with a functioning brain had a prescheduled sale of stock, and could have it coincide with the biggest positive news story in the world, what do you think the person would do? Not to abuse an internet trope, but truly, they think you're stupid.

Notably, the data was incredibly positive, and took account of ninety-four confirmed cases in the study—nearly three times the original interim analysis threshold. This means they had clearly eclipsed the thirty-two-case threshold well before election day, as they had previously expected.

President Trump called it out for what it was right away. He tweeted, "As I have long said, @Pfizer and the others would only announce a Vaccine after the Election, because they didn't have the courage to do it before. Likewise, the @US_FDA should have announced it earlier, not for political purposes, but for saving lives!"

Of course, the media and the "fact checkers" sprang into action to call Trump a liar and confirm the absurd notion that the timing was just a coincidence.[19] They gave all deference to Bourla, who said on Monday, November 9, "I learned about those results yesterday, Sunday, at 2:00. And the independent experts' committee, independent from Pfizer, that unblinded the data and reviewed, they met at 11 and they finished their meeting at 1:30."[20] The press even printed his pithy quote that Pfizer moved "at the speed of science." How quaint.

Of course, all of that ignores the fact that Pfizer and the FDA literally changed the rules and decided to wait to look at the data at the behest of Biden's campaign. "I learned about those results yesterday," Bourla said. Yes, because he chose to wait—not because the data only became available on that day.

Pfizer even further raised suspicion among the Trump team, who had tried to work constructively with the vaccine companies throughout Operation Warp Speed. The company informed the Biden team of the data release in advance of the public announcement and let the sitting administration find out in the press.

Then, in spite of their prior "distrust" of the vaccines for political purposes, both Joe Biden and Kamala Harris received vaccinations in December of 2020.[21]

Just in case there is any doubt as to whether or not the timing of the data announcement was a coincidence, consider some other relevant facts. First, in July 2020, President Trump signed a series of executive orders to lower the price of prescription drugs in America.[22] Albert Bourla came out forcefully against it.[23] One of the first acts of the Biden administration was to freeze and scrutinize Trump's policies implemented by the Department of Health and Human Services.[24] Whose team do you think Pfizer was on in this scenario?

Additionally, Pfizer donated $1 million to Biden's inaugural committee, and campaign contributors connected to Pfizer donated more than three times as much to Biden as they did to Trump.[25],[26] Pfizer's head of government affairs and their political action committee also happens—coincidentally, I'm sure—to be a Democrat political appointee from the Clinton administration.

Then, after the Biden administration came into office in 2021, they gave Pfizer a massive, multi-billion-dollar windfall. In 2020, the Trump administration negotiated to purchase millions and millions of doses of the coronavirus vaccine, for Americans, for $19.50 per dose. In the summer of 2021, after all Americans had access to vaccines, the Biden administration purchased five hundred million additional doses from Pfizer for the purpose of shipping them overseas to other countries, including sub-Saharan Africa.[27]

We can debate whether the U.S. government should be so generous, but we cannot debate whether that purchase made the most sense—because it obviously didn't. Pfizer's vaccines famously require highly complex packaging with extraordinarily cold storage in order to remain effective, and such storage does not exist in many of the countries to which it was being shipped.[28] In addition to more durable options, there were obviously less expensive ones available as well. While it has a lower efficacy rate than Pfizer, the Johnson & Johnson vaccine is easier to store and costs about one-fourth of the price per individual vaccinated. The J&J shot is a one-dose shot and costs only $10, instead of about $40 per individual vaccinated with the Pfizer vaccine.[29]

Shortly after this massive purchase, which made little sense, the Biden administration made an additional purchase of two hundred million Pfizer vaccines and offered a higher price of $24 per dose, or $48 per individual—over a 20 percent markup from the original price.[30]

The motive in this case is clear.

This entire episode was infuriating. Pfizer, the Biden campaign, and the FDA obviously rigged the system. The press let them get away with it. Biden might have won the election because of it. Pfizer got a handsome payoff as a result. What's more, many families might have suffered unnecessarily because of it.

The public truly deserves to know the truth, and families whose loved ones have died because of any delay in the approval process should be compensated. An enterprising plaintiff's attorney might even locate some of those families and offer to represent them. The lawyer would need to identify only plaintiffs whose family members contracted the virus during the eighteen-day delay before the FDA's approval on December 11, 2020. At that time, one to two thousand people per day were dying of the coronavirus. It certainly appears as though tens of thousands of people may have died because of political influence on science. If anyone does bring such a case, discovery would be fascinating and could lead to justice for many Americans.

Simple Salad Dressing, BY TERESA

With a chapter about vaccines and the FDA, the least we could do is write a healthy detox recipe. This salad dressing is the star of the show here, and it's a staple in our refrigerator. It's healthy and perfectly balanced, and can go with pretty much any salad. There's a detoxifying factor to it as well due to the apple cider vinegar, so it will make you feel like a better person!

MAKES ABOUT ½ CUP

1 garlic clove, crushed
2 Tbsp. Dijon mustard
¼ cup olive oil
¼ cup apple cider vinegar
Juice from 1 lemon
2 Tbsp. honey
Salt and pepper to taste

Whisk together all the ingredients except the honey. Then add in the honey. Whisk again until emulsified. Add salt and pepper to taste.

Serve over any salad mixture of your choice. I prefer this combination, mixed in a bowl:

Romaine lettuce   Cucumber slices
Baby arugula   Sliced almonds
Shredded carrots   Pomegranate seeds
Cherry tomatoes

It will leave you feeling refreshed and ready to tackle any challenge.

TO DRINK

Gin Fizz, BY BRIAN

This is a light and refreshing drink that goes with nearly anything, so it seems like a natural pairing for a salad with Teresa's dressing.

    2 oz. gin
    ½ oz. simple syrup
    ½ oz. lemon juice
    1 to 2 oz. soda water (seltzer)
    1 egg white (optional)
    1 lemon twist (optional, for garnish)

If you want to make this cocktail the simple way, without an egg white, then pour all the other ingredients over ice, stir, and enjoy. If you want to make it the way a fancy cocktail bar would, then put the gin, simple syrup, lemon juice, and egg white in a shaker with ice and shake it thoroughly for a good 15 to 30 seconds. Then pour the frothy mix into a glass, top with the soda water, stir gently, and put a lemon twist on the rim for garnish.

CHAPTER 16

"A Different Kind of a Guy"

BY BRIAN

In the final months of the Trump administration, a number of us maintained a laser focus on Operation Warp Speed and vaccinations. We met almost daily in the Roosevelt Room of the White House. The informal group included senior advisor and presidential son-in-law Jared Kushner, Paul Mango from the Department of Health and Human Services, Dr. Deborah Birx from the Coronavirus Task Force, Adam Boehler, head of the U.S. International Development Finance Corporation and a board member of Operation Warp Speed, and a rotating cast of other senior administration officials.

At the time, I was receiving questions constantly from members of the White House press corps regarding if and when President Trump would be vaccinated.

Jared thought it was a fair question, and that since the president had recovered from COVID already and had natural immunity, the point was really to show the American people that they should have confidence in the vaccines, rather than to demonstrate the potential immunity benefits. So we started brainstorming potential scenarios in which the president could receive the vaccine in a public way.

One of the ideas was to have the president invite the former presidents to the White House—or to some other site—to have all of them receive the vaccine together in a show of unity. I don't recall how it was decided, but one way or another, it was decided that Cassidy Luna, who worked in Jared's office, and I would talk to President Trump about it and gauge his interest.

We walked into his private study off the Oval Office, which warrants describing.

There is a door in the Oval Office to the president's left as he sits at the Resolute desk. Through the door is a hallway. As you enter the hallway, immediately on the right is his private restroom. Across from the restroom is what some of us referred to as "the store" and the president referred to as the Lewinsky Room, for reasons we don't need to discuss in this book. In this room were shelves full of interesting gifts that the president would give to people who visited him. I have a great collection of cufflinks, a MAGA hat, and challenge coins.

At the end of the hallway is a dining room. President Trump converted it into his private office. The table was always stacked high with papers, as was his custom even in his office in Trump Tower in New York. But the most interesting things in that room were the gifts. People sent the president gifts from all over the country.

The room is warm and inviting, with a fireplace and a beautiful crystal chandelier. The president typically sat at the end of the table closest to the door and the window to the outside, across from the fireplace. Outside this room is a narrow stone pathway that leads down to an alcove sitting area, and farther down the path is the first family's private pool, which is well-concealed behind beautiful greenery.

As I was saying, the president typically sat at the end of the table closest to the windows, facing the fireplace. A TV was mounted on the wall above the fireplace—usually tuned to Fox News.

On the mantel, he had football helmets, a folded American flag in a wooden case, two signed footballs, a miniature model of the White House, and a clock. Above the TV were two massive gold belts mounted on the wall—one with the World Boxing Council (WBC) seal and another with the Ultimate Fighting Championship (UFC) seal. The UFC belt was almost surely a gift from his friend and supporter Dana White, president of that organization.

To the right over the doorway hung another enormous gold wrestling belt—one custom-made that said "Donald Trump" above a small presidential seal and the phrase "Make America Great Again." Lest we forget, before he was president, Donald Trump was a member of the WWE Hall of Fame.

To the right of the door hung a portrait of President Theodore Roosevelt, below which sat a bronze model of Mount Rushmore with Trump's bust added next to Abraham Lincoln's. To the right of that was a painting of Republican presidents smiling and laughing around a table, with President Trump most prominently featured. The other presidents around the table were Lincoln, Reagan, both Bushes, Eisenhower, Teddy Roosevelt, Nixon, Ford, and Coolidge.

On the other side of the room were exquisite historic paintings and photographs, including an iconic shot of the president and first lady slow dancing in the Grand Foyer of the White House.

It was in this room that Press Secretary Kayleigh McEnany and I went to speak with Trump after Joe Biden had announced that he was choosing Kamala Harris to be his running mate. The president wanted to do a press conference, where he would surely comment on that massive bit of political news of the day, and he wanted to speak with us about what else the press was covering that day. As the president edited his prepared remarks, I recall him asking, "Should I say that Kamala is Joe

Biden's running mate, or should I call him 'Sleepy Joe'?" I laughed out loud, and immediately said, "Well, I laughed." He went with Sleepy Joe.

But back to this story. Cassidy and I walked into the president's study, where he was seated in his usual spot. We said that we wanted to get his thoughts on getting vaccinated in a public way to promote vaccine confidence. The team wanted to gauge his interest in an event with all of the former presidents, during which he and they would be vaccinated together. He made a face that conveyed, shall we say, a healthy skepticism. He said, "I'll get the shot. Do they want me to get the shot? I'll get the shot." But regarding an event with the former presidents, he said: "Nah, I'm a different kind of a guy, ya know?" Then he reiterated that he would be happy to get vaccinated but asked us to think about other event ideas, and we went on our way.

Ultimately, the president received a vaccine shortly before leaving the White House, but he did so privately.

That comment, "I'm a different kind of a guy," struck me for a number of reasons. First, perhaps truer words were never spoken. There's no one else quite like Donald Trump. Second, he really was a different kind of president. He rose to power on his celebrity and connection with audiences, not on a political or military career. He also famously trashed presidents of both parties, the Establishment, and the "swamp" throughout his run and his presidency. He was the candidate who lamented the state of the "system" and then wound up in charge of it. He is indeed a "different kind of a guy."

Mediterranean Date Chicken, BY TERESA

How about pairing a story about a "different kind of a guy" with a different kind of dinner? This dish was inspired by one I used to make with the help of Blue Apron, but I've changed the protein and put my own spin on it.

SERVES 2

2 chicken breasts
Salt and pepper to taste
¼ cup rice flour
2 Tbsp. smoked paprika
1 tsp. ras el hanout
2 Tbsp. butter
2 cloves garlic, minced
4 dates, pitted and chopped
Lemon wedge
2 Tbsp. roasted almonds, chopped

Pat the chicken breasts dry, then salt and pepper each side. In a separate shallow bowl, mix the rice flour, paprika, and ras el hanout. Coat each chicken breast with the flour mixture. In a nonstick pan, cook the chicken breasts over medium-high heat about 5 minutes on each side. After the chicken is done cooking, turn the heat to low. Add the butter, garlic, dates, and a tablespoon of water. Once the butter is melted, spoon the sauce over the chicken. Plate the chicken and pour the sauce over it. Squeeze a lemon wedge generously over the chicken. Top with chopped almonds.

TO DRINK

Gin Martini with a Twist, BY BRIAN

This was a go-to drink when my colleagues and I worked late on the Tax Cuts and Jobs Act and went out for a cocktail to wind down. It was introduced to the gang by my great friend Tricia McLaughlin, who worked with me at the Treasury Department. The bottom line is this: Olives are disgusting. Martinis are not. Act accordingly. Oh, and Hendrick's Gin tastes best, but there are plenty of good ones out there.

2 to 2½ oz. gin
½ to 1 oz. dry vermouth
1 lemon or orange twist

Put ice cubes in a shaker. Add the gin and vermouth, and shake well. Strain into a glass. Twist a lemon rind or piece of orange zest over the glass (or use a lemon slice or an orange slice if you want more citrus flavor), and drop it in for garnish. Oh, and don't let olives anywhere near this drink.

CHAPTER 17

Final Conversation with the President in the Oval Office

BY BRIAN

In the waning days of the administration, the staff remaining in each office took group photos with President Trump in the Oval Office. When it was the Office of Communications' turn, l led the group from the Roosevelt Room across the hall into the Oval through a door to the president's left as he sat at the Resolute desk. We formed a semicircle behind the president. Shealah Craighead, the intrepid and always good-natured White House photographer, snapped a series of photos, and then we went around the front of the desk to chat with the president before the next group was scheduled to enter.

By that time, the president had been banned from certain social media sites (including Twitter), and so his first question directed at me was, "Are our statements still getting out there?" I responded that yes, every statement was tweeted and retweeted instantly by thousands upon thousands of journalists and citizens alike. He commented that in a way, he felt liberated not having to constantly tweet; while he didn't actually say "tweet," he made a motion as though he were typing on a smartphone.

President Trump is one of many victims of cancel culture that the left has effectively limited or silenced because of their political views. Of course, leftists have yet to cancel enemies of the United States like the Ayatollah or apparatchiks of the Chinese Communist Party, which says an unfortunate amount about the American left and its priorities. Now Trump is suing the social media companies and has launched his own platform called Truth Social to push back on the unfair status quo.

In the office that day, the president began asking where we thought the media environment would be heading once he left office, and in light of his being banned from Twitter and other sites. I answered that cable news might never be the same, if it even survived another decade in its current form. Trump had been single-handedly responsible for off-the-charts cable news ratings ever since he started running for president in 2015. In his absence, the outrage business would not be nearly as successful. Additionally, the fragmentation of our society due to social media algorithms that generate self-assuring content to reinforce—and not challenge—beliefs meant that unifying the country was becoming more difficult. A number of other staff members discussed ratings and various statistics, and the president listened intently.

Then President Trump went down the row of staffers asking if each person had found a job yet and if there was anything he could do to help. Several had landed positions on Capitol Hill, while some of us were searching and/or mulling over various options.

When it was time for the next group of staff members to enter the room, our team began walking out through the opposite door from where we had entered, to the president's right towards the "Outer Oval," where his personal assistant and others were seated.

One of my colleagues discreetly asked the president to sign a photo of the two of them, which he did enthusiastically. Then the president pointed at me and said, "If there's anything I can do for you, let me know.

You want a letter of recommendation? If you want one, write up a draft [motioning as if he were writing]. Write whatever you want. Write whatever you want and I'll sign it [motioning again]."

I said okay, thanked him for everything, and walked out.

The next day I sent a draft to the staff secretary's office and asked for it to be put in front of the president, noting that he had told me himself that he wanted to sign it. The office never responded. Though I'm sure they had plenty of things on their plate, that always irked me. In truth, I would probably just would have framed a recommendation and hung it on the wall. But that was one last example of how many of the staff had ignored the president's wishes. Very frustrating.

Fresh Tomato-Pasta Salad, BY BRIAN

After we concluded our service at the White House in January, Teresa and I hopped on a plane and jetted off to St. Lucia for a beautiful tropical vacation. So naturally, a light and summery dish makes sense here. Enter my mom's delicious tomato-pasta salad, a perfect snack for the beach or a picnic.

SERVES 8

4 to 6 fresh tomatoes
½ to ⅔ cup olive oil
¼ cup red wine vinegar
2 garlic cloves, minced
Salt and pepper to taste
12 oz. bowtie pasta
4 to 6 basil leaves
Shredded mozzarella and/or Parmesan

Blanch, peal, and chop the fresh tomatoes. Mix them in a bowl with the olive oil, red wine vinegar, garlic, and salt and pepper to taste.

Boil the pasta in salted water until al dente, rinse, and drain.

Put the pasta in a serving bowl. Add the tomato mixture and the fresh basil. Add a dusting of shredded mozzarella and/or Parmesan and mix thoroughly. Top with another light coating of cheese. Let sit for about 15 minutes at room temperature, then chill in the refrigerator.

TO DRINK

Winterguard, BY BRIAN

This recipe is really courtesy of my sister Cindy, who was generous enough to let me publish it. It was passed to her by friends over the years. In any event, it's called Winterguard because nobody would drink something called Anti-freeze. But that's the point—to have a highly alcoholic, delicious tropical drink that will warm you up in the winter, so this cocktail seems fitting since we went to St. Lucia in January after leaving the White House.

MAKES A LARGE PITCHER OR PUNCH BOWL'S WORTH

16 oz. freshly squeezed lemon juice
8 oz. freshly squeezed orange juice
8 oz. orgeat syrup
2 oz. vodka
2 oz. brandy
13 oz. white wine, preferably sweet, like a Riesling
39 oz. white rum
8 oz. water
Lemon or orange slices, for garnish
Maraschino or amaretto cherries, for garnish

Blend all of the ingredients except the fruit slices and cherries in a large pitcher or punch bowl and chill in the refrigerator. Serve over ice, garnished with the fruit.

Warning: Do not drive or operate heavy machinery after drinking Winter-guard. Our uncle almost got a DUI after one glass. When my sister Katie and I wrapped Christmas presents after drinking it one year on Christmas Eve, no one could understand the gift tags in the morning. So enjoy but proceed with caution.

CHAPTER 18

Will He or Won't He Run?

BY BRIAN

One of the most asked but not yet answered questions is: Will Donald Trump run for president again, or will he anoint a successor?

In the waning days of our time in the White House, we launched an initiative called the 1776 Commission. President Trump signed an executive order creating an entity composed of scholars dedicated to preserving our nation's character and history. It was partly a response to the 1619 Project, which promotes a disgraceful and inaccurate account of American history, and views everything in America through the poisonous prism of racism. As part of the 1776 Commission's launch, we hosted a meeting of its members in the Cabinet Room at the White House. The Cabinet Room is in the West Wing between the Oval Office and the James S. Brady Press Briefing Room.

The Domestic Policy Council was serving as the organizing office of the commission, and the council staff asked me to speak to the members about what to expect in terms of press coverage and give them my advice.

Before the president arrived at the meeting, I told them that we might or might not invite the press corps into the room, but that the commissioners could expect questions from the press one way or another. The members of the commission had been chosen for a reason. Or rather, they had been chosen for their work, experience, and patriotism. They could answer questions or not at their discretion, but they had to be aware that certain outlets would treat them fairly and others would not. Those of us in the White House press office were there to assist them as needed and to ensure that any answers to media questions were accurate and consistent.

My comments that day were not particularly insightful or memorable. However, President Trump's were. He was scheduled to enter the room, read some brief prepared comments, thank the members for their willingness to serve, and return to the Oval Office to attend to the day's business.

Trump has never been a rule follower. He proceeded to enter the room and speak with the group for about an hour. He spoke about how poorly the election had been managed at the state level and how dark forces were working hard on the left. He encouraged the commission to research election integrity and its impact on our democracy.

A member of the Commission said that perhaps it was a blessing that Trump had not come out on top in this contest—that if he had won, he would face the difficulties of every second-term president, which included fatigue.

Two-term presidencies typically deal with a brutal combination of criticism from the opposition party and distancing by the incumbent party candidates for president, hoping to be seen as their own man (or woman), rather than merely a continuation of the previous administration.

Another member of the commission said that if President Trump were to come back to run in the next election, he could win in a landslide and cement his legacy.

In response, Trump pointed at me and said, "I'm not [Brian's] age." He went on to say that perhaps he would not have the same energy level that he had when he started running in 2015. We were talking about four years into the future, and a national election requires tremendous stamina, traveling across the country on a day-to-day basis holding rallies to turn out voters.

Now, having observed him on the campaign trail and his continued involvement in politics at every level, I believe it seems more likely than not that Trump intends to run again and that he can win. Remember, I accompanied him on that campaign fundraising swing to the east end of Long Island. In blue Long Island—of all places—people lined the streets for miles cheering, holding signs, and snapping pictures of the motorcade, just hoping for a glimpse of or a wave from "45." It was the same in many places we visited, from Minnesota to Iowa to Arizona—to every corner of the nation. To quote Russell Crowe playing Roger Ailes in the movie *The Loudest Voice*, "People f*cking love Donald Trump."

Mojo Steak, BY BRIAN AND TERESA

Since this story is about President Trump's mojo (pronounced "moe-joe"), or ability to win again, let's make some mojo (pronounced "moe-hoe") steak, especially since any victory might be due to the Republicans' growing popularity with the Hispanic population. This recipe was inspired by Brian's college roommate Jorge, who makes an absolutely delicious mojo steak.

SERVES 6

2 lbs. thin, boneless flank steak
4 cloves garlic, minced
2 cups orange juice
1 cup lime juice
3 cups mojo marinade (available in the international section of most grocery stores)
1 Tbsp. salt
2 tsp. black pepper

Cut several lines in the meat so that the sauce will sink in when you marinate it. Mix all of the ingredients except the meat into a sealable plastic bag, seal it, and shake it up. Put the meat in the bag and reseal it. Put the bag in the refrigerator and let it sit overnight if you can, but for at least 2 hours.

Heat a grill to 400°F. Put the meat on the grill and close the lid. Cook it for about 4 minutes. Flip it and cook for another 4 minutes. If you're using a meat thermometer, the meat should be about 135°F. Take the meat off the grill and let it sit for about 5 minutes. Once it's ready, slice into thin pieces and serve. Tip: This goes well with a light, summery salad.

Coco-jito (Coconut Mojito), BY TERESA

1 cup water
1 cup sugar
4 sprigs fresh mint, divided
2 oz. coconut rum
1 oz. lime juice
3 oz. coconut water

In a pot, add the water, sugar, and 3 sprigs of mint, and bring to a boil. Let cool. You should now have a minty simple syrup. Put ice in a shaker. Pour in the coconut rum, lime juice, and coconut water. Add 1 oz. of the minty simple syrup. (The rest can be saved for future use.) Shake well. Pour into a glass and garnish with a sprig of mint. Optional: You can top this off with soda water for some additional fizz.

CHAPTER 19

Mean Tweets

BY BRIAN

I would be remiss if I published stories about my time in the White House and didn't include some of the best mean tweets sent in my direction. Without further ado, here are some of my favorites.

"Yesman douchebucket" was perhaps the most creative and interesting description in the mean tweets. I'm not sure what I did or said during a CNN interview to trigger the ire of @HerronIsland, but whatever it was compelled her to tweet on September 21, 2020, ".@BMorgenstern45 was on CNN this morning. What a yesman douchebucket." It's just so crisp. I have to say I'm impressed.

I knew I'd made it when Montel Williams sh*t-talked to me on Twitter. On September 4, 2020, he wrote, "@BMorgenstern45 Brian – I realize your job is to prostitute yourself for Donald...Having known him for 20+ years, it won't turn out well for you."

I didn't respond. But my saved draft read, "Didn't expect to check 'get trash talked by Montel Williams' off the bucket list today but here we are. Can't wait to tune into your next payday loan infomercial." It wasn't my best work. It's probably best that I didn't click send.

I was also intrigued when the creator of some of my favorite movies, Judd Apatow, got in on the action. On October 5, 2020, I tweeted very bland, factual information about coronavirus contact tracing. Four days later @JuddApatow wrote, "Shame on you for protecting a President who has killed tens of thousands of additional people in order to help himself politically. He has clearly lost his mind and is infecting people personally and for a buck U help him continue his evil murderous behavior. You are part of it."

I'm not really sure where to begin with this one. President Trump had assembled Operation Warp Speed to develop vaccines five times faster than ever before, shut down our economy, shut down travel with China and Europe, and made many other difficult decisions to save quite literally millions of lives. So accusing him of mass murder is a tough sell. Also, thinking that somehow mass murder would *help* politically is quite a take. Looping me into the mass murder accusation is, well, a ridiculous thing to do. Whatever. I still think *Anchorman* is hilarious.

Speaking of *Anchorman*...

Also impressive was the hatred with which people reacted to even the friendliest and most innocuous of tweets. For example, on November 16, 2020, I quote-tweeted a *Wall Street Journal* story about the extraordinary effectiveness of the Moderna coronavirus vaccine, stating, "President @realDonaldTrump's #OperationWarpSpeed is helping to bring vaccines to market faster than ever before. GREAT NEWS that Moderna's Covid vaccine is showing over 94% efficacy!"

The first reply was from someone named @JanuaryHandl, who wrote, "You will meet your maker with the blood of your fellow humans all over your hands. How dare you?"

I was a little confused by the question mark. I read it in my mind the way Will Ferrell playing Ron Burgundy in *Anchorman* read his own name when someone put a question mark after it in the teleprompter.

On Christmas Eve I tweeted, "Merry Christmas & God Bless America." The first response, on Christmas Eve, from @Elisabethmngirl, who had Christmas tree emojis in her Twitter name, was "Gross. This administration is a disgrace. May every single person associated be shunned."

And good tidings to you, ma'am.

I think the most fun exchange was with the former FBI agent and now infamous Peter Strzok. On September 4, 2020, he (strangely) tweeted a picture of my then Twitter profile, stating, "Hi @bmorgentsern45, happy to have become one of your/WH Communication Office's 309 official follows last night. Glad the WH is finally paying attention to @realDonaldTrump's disrespect to our fallen soldiers." He was apparently referring to the oft-debunked *Atlantic* story about President Trump's allegedly saying disparaging things about long-dead World War I veterans. At least twenty-seven witnesses came out and said that the article was completely bogus, but hey, it wouldn't be past Peter to accuse the president of something he hadn't done. I responded accordingly.

I tweeted him, "Are you going to try to frame me for a crime I didn't commit, too? Give my best to Lisa." (Lisa was a reference to his coworker and mistress Lisa Page.)

I could go on about mean tweets for a while, but I'll stop there with a win and wish all the haters and losers, of which there are many, a pleasant day.

General T's Chicken, BY TERESA

A story about spicy tweets pairs well with a spicy chicken recipe. Brian always says that if he were forced to eat one meal for the rest of his life, it would be Buffalo chicken. Then I made this for him, and he said it might take Buffalo chicken's place. I hope you'll enjoy it too!

SERVES 2

½ cup soy sauce
1 Tbsp. rice vinegar
2 Tbsp. gochujang
1 Tbsp. honey
1 tsp. hot sesame oil (can be found in international markets)
1 Tbsp. brown sugar
2 tsp. ginger, minced
2 cloves garlic, minced
2 tsp. ginger powder, divided
2 tsp. garlic powder, divided
2 chicken breasts, chopped into cubes
Salt and pepper to taste
½ cup flour
Olive oil
Rice or other grain, for serving
Sesame seeds (optional, for garnish)
Green onions, sliced (optional. for garnish)

(continued)

Whisk together the soy sauce, rice vinegar, gochujang, honey, sesame oil, brown sugar, ginger, garlic, ginger powder, and 1 tsp. garlic powder until blended well. Season the chicken with 1 tsp. garlic powder, salt, and pepper. Toss the chicken in the flour.

Coat a nonstick pan with olive oil. When the oil is hot (test with flour to see if it sizzles), cook the chicken thoroughly, about 4 minutes on each side depending on thickness. Once the chicken is cooked, add in the sauce. Cook for another 2 to 3, minutes ensuring the chicken is thoroughly coated.

Serve over a bed of rice or another grain of your choice. Add a garnish such as sesame seeds or chopped green onion, and serve.

TO DRINK

Aunt Inez' Punch, BY BRIAN

My great-great aunt Inez was known as a firecracker, and her favorite sweet punch pairs well with a spicy dish. In the early '80s in northern New Jersey, when I was just a baby, she was a little old lady with a big personality. She wore a three-diamond ring on her pinkie, and her hair was piled high on top of her head. She drove a robin's-egg-blue Mercury Comet. She was exceedingly short, so neighborhood boys helped her out by duct-taping wooden blocks to the pedals in her car so she could reach them. When she drove, people could see the top of her head poking out over the steering wheel, and her diamond pinkie ring. She would drive over to a restaurant and bar called the Homestead and play the piano for the folks. She also liked to throw parties and would serve her favorite punch—which, well, packs a punch! Note: This recipe makes enough for a group of people.

MAKES MORE THAN A GALLON

9 oz. frozen lemonade
3 cups brandy
6 cups light rum
4 oz. peach schnapps
6 to 8 cups club soda
Preferred fruit, for garnish

Combine the ingredients in a large pitcher or punch bowl and chill. Serve over ice and garnish with fruit.

CHAPTER 20

White House Vaccine Summit

BY TERESA

One of the projects I'm most proud of in my career is Operation Warp Speed—the project to develop and manufacture a safe and effective vaccine for COVID-19. For the first time in history, a vaccine was developed and manufactured in only nine months. Having a front row seat to the work done by the scientific community, the military community, the federal government, and the private sector was awe-inspiring and special. This, along with the greatest mobilization of resources since World War II to help combat COVID-19 made me feel like I was part of something monumental and historic.

I joined the White House from the Pentagon because of my knowledge of the Department of Defense. The military was responsible for coordinating the logistics for manufacturing and delivery of the eventually approved COVID-19 vaccine. We had a great team, and what made it extra special was that I got to work closely with Brian. As it turned out, we were one of several couples that worked together in the White House.

The COVID-19 communications team worked closely with the staff, doctors, generals, and scientists at the Department of Health and Human

Services, the Pentagon, and the COVID-19 task force. It was an honor to learn from these leaders and work with them. And a lot of intelligent people in one room can lead to interesting conversations!

As we got closer to an approved vaccine from several candidates going through trials, we wanted the American public to understand that this vaccine was safe and effective. It was the hope everyone needed to turn the corner on the coronavirus pandemic. But getting that message out with a hostile media environment proved to be more difficult than it needed to be.

Jared Kushner, who was an integral part of Operation Warp Speed, came up with a brilliant idea to hold a vaccine summit to show the American people a behind-the-scenes look at what was going into developing the vaccine in record time. It would be an all-day event that would bring together the communities that were working on the vaccine and would include several presentations and remarks, while being streamed live on several cable networks. We had major companies like UPS, McKesson, Walgreens, and CVS represented. We garnered support from members of Congress to write op-eds and attend in person. Several of the major players from Operation Warp Speed were also in attendance and gave presentations, including Dr. Deborah Birx, Dr. Francis Collins (director of the National Institutes of Health), Secretary Alex Azar, Surgeon General Jerome Adams, and more. Several cabinet secretaries attended, and of course, the president and the vice president delivered remarks and applauded the entire project. The only person who didn't attend was Dr. Fauci, who we were told was too busy accepting an award. Turns out he was attending an event for Joe Biden. In case anyone had doubts as to whether Fauci is a Democrat, this should confirm it.

As we approached the date of the summit, in early December 2020, several members of the press and communications teams either were unfortunately sick with COVID or had left the White House for the private sector, postelection vacations, or other new horizons. It left us with a skeleton crew of just me, Brian, and a handful of junior staff working on this event. Brian and I were doing double duty to make sure we had a good communications plan in place to get maximum exposure for the summit.

We developed strategic communications planning memos, which we called "tick tocks," so that Operation Warp Speed's message spread far and wide through print, TV, and radio with a regular cadence. The strategy documents didn't come easy, though. With so many different principals (the cabinet secretaries and VIPs), we had to think about how to give each some airtime without stepping on anyone's toes. And with the thin staff, it was left to Brian and me to brainstorm and put the plan together.

We worked long hours at the White House and went home together late at night to continue our work. Since we lived together, we could easily keep working on the plan. In addition to our planning, we had to coordinate with several external teams to ensure that schedules lined up and principals (the bosses) were happy with their placements. We set up media rows on the White House grounds so that the principals could easily go from one media outlet to the next. We pitched preview stories to the White House press corps and gave exclusives to a few print reporters. We strategized on booking more than thirty TV hits for more than fifteen people. It was not an easy two-person job, but we got it done.

The vaccine summit was a hit. It received great exposure, and it was the first time an event at the White House went off (mostly) without any drama, hitches or, quite frankly, negative press. It was a solid event that displayed the talents of all the people behind it and Operation Warp Speed. Many high-level principals came out of it impressed and happy. Brian and I personally felt very proud and accomplished.

As we worked through long hours together, I was reminded of two things. The first time Brian and I were stuck together in one room working was during the beginning of the pandemic. I thought of how Brian had been glued to his computer for long hours implementing the CARES Act. This time, though, I was right by his side, asking him questions and double-checking our work. We learned how to work together and created a pretty good balance of being coworkers and future spouses.

I was also reminded of how blessed I was to share this White House experience with my best friend. The White House is a tough environment to work in, and I couldn't have done it without him. We have a trust that is very rare in those hallways. And that partnership especially got us through the tough outcome of the election and moving on to new jobs.

Most people say they would never work with their spouse (I most certainly said this once). I've come to discover that your greatest teammate can also be the love of your life.

Linguini Carbonara, BY TERESA

Carbonara is one of our favorite sauces, and so it pairs perfectly with a proud memory that we shared together. It seems daunting to make, but if you time it right, you can get a creamy, delicious sauce in a matter of seconds.

SERVES 4

12 oz. (1 box) linguine
Olive oil
2 cloves garlic, minced
½ lb. prosciutto, diced
2 egg yolks
1½ cups freshly grated Parmesan, divided
Salt and pepper, to taste

Heat a pot of heavily salted water and bring it to a boil. Begin cooking the pasta according to the instructions on the box, or at least until al dente. Meanwhile, in a pan, heat a layer of olive oil over medium-high heat. Add in the garlic and cook until fragrant. Add in the prosciutto and cook until crispy.

While the garlic and the prosciutto are cooking, mix together the egg yolks and 1 cup Parmesan thoroughly in a separate bowl until blended.

When the pasta is done cooking, drain it, reserving 1 cup pasta water. Transfer the drained pasta to the pot with the garlic and prosciutto.

Turn off the heat and remove the pan to an unused burner. Pour in the egg-and-Parmesan sauce, using tongs to mix and blend the sauce and the pasta together. Add in the pasta water in increments to help bind the sauce. Add salt and pepper to taste, then add in more Parmesan to top it off. Serve while warm.

TO DRINK

White Wine with Dinner; Limoncello Slushy for Dessert, BY BRIAN

Many people would say that a classic Italian red wine like a chianti pairs well with carbonara, but we prefer a lighter white with this rich dish. Robert Mondavi makes a nice sauvignon blanc and pinot grigio.

Then it's time to top off the decadent meal with an absolutely incredible dessert cocktail—the limoncello slushy. It's a favorite of Brian's mom's (and everyone else who tastes it).

SERVES ABOUT 4 SLUSHIES

1 pint lemon sorbet (or vanilla ice cream for a richer taste)
6 oz. Champagne or prosecco
4 oz. limoncello (or limoncello with cream)

Put all the ingredients in a blender and blend for 10 to 15 seconds. Pour into a Champagne glass and serve with a straw.

Acknowledgments

We wrote this book because we found ourselves in unimaginable circumstances, and we made it through together, with good humor and delicious food. We could not have done it without the love, support, and sarcasm of our parents and siblings. So to Bob and Nancy Morgenstern, Bill and Kim Davis, Daniel and Rosalia Cannatella, Cindy and Greg Daly, John and Alison Morgenstern, Katie Morton, and our nephews and nieces Brian and Anna Morgenstern, Aurelia and Daniel Cannatella, Jr., and Alex Morton, we hope this effort makes you proud.

We also want to say a special thank you to Tony Sayegh for being an all-around great friend and mentor, and for making sure we met that fateful night in 2018. Thank you also to Katie Pavlich and Morgan Ortagus for being born! (And for being terrific people.) We met at your birthday party and are so glad to be your friends. We would also be remiss if we did not also thank several other of our bosses and friends who made it all happen, including and especially: President Donald Trump; Secretaries Steven Mnuchin, Mike Pompeo, Wilbur Ross, and Mark Esper; Assistant Secretary Marie Royce; Jared Kushner; Alyssa Farah Griffin for helping to hire us to the White House; and the inimitable Kayleigh McEnany.

Endnotes

1   Denise Grady and Katie Thomas, "Coronavirus Vaccine: Moderna and Pfizer Reveal Secret Blueprints Trials," *New York Times*, September 17, 2020, updated November 16, 2020.

2   "National Vaccine Injury Compensation Program: Rescission of Revisions to the Vaccine Injury Table," Federal Register, April 22, 2021.

3   Ezekiel Emanuel and Paul Offit, "Could Trump Turn a Vaccine Into a Campaign Stunt?" *New York Times*, June 8, 2020.

4   Ezekiel Emanuel, "Why I Hope to Die at 75," *The Atlantic*, October 2014.

5   *Today Show*, "Pfizer CEO on Coronavirus Vaccine: 'We Will Have an Answer by the End of October,'" TODAY.com.

6   Lauren Egan, "Harris on vaccine: 'I would not trust Donald Trump,'" NBCNews.com, September 5, 2020.

7   Candy Morrison, "Biden does not trust Trump to deliver a safe vaccine," *Washington Examiner*, September 29, 2020.

8   "6 Days After Letter From 65 Top Health Experts, Pfizer Backs Off October Vaccine Prediction."
    Adam Cancryn and Sarah Owermohle, "Pfizer trying to defuse critics amid push for vaccine before Election Day," Politico, October 9, 2020—quote from that article: "Pfizer has also set up a one-on-one briefing between Bourla and Ezekiel Emanuel, an adviser to Joe Biden, after he organized a widely circulated letter urging the company to hold off on seeking any vaccine authorization until 'at least late November.'"
    Sarah Owermohle, "Pfizer delivers final blow to Trump's hope for preelection vaccine," Politico via Yahoo News, October 16, 2020—quote from that article: "Emanuel penned a letter to Pfizer this month with dozens of scientists raising concerns."
    Wesley J. Smith, "Ezekiel Emanuel Wants to Shut Down the Country Again," National Review, July 27, 2020—quote from that article: "Of course, the ultimate impact of such a course would almost surely be the election of—no coincidence—Joe Biden. So, one suspects this is a letter more steeped in political machinations than epidemiological analysis."

9   Licensure and Emergency Use Authorization of Vaccines to Prevent Covid-19: Clinical Considerations," accessed November 11, 2021.

10 Paul Mango, *Warp Speed: Inside the Operation that Beat Covid, the Critics, and the Odds*, (New York, NY: Republic Book Publishers, 2022): pp.126–128.

11 Ed Silverman, "Ezekiel Emanuel on Covid-19 vaccines and a failed U.S. response," STAT, October 13, 2020—quote from that article: "I explained to them what I thought the problem was in terms of communications.... I told them they could do a press release or other things so it's clear."

12 Sarah Owermohle, "Pfizer delivers final blow to Trump's hope for preelection vaccine," Politico via Yahoo News, October 16, 2020.

13 Paul Mango, *Warp Speed: Inside the Operation that Beat Covid, the Critics, and the Odds*.

14 "Pfizer and BioNTech Announce Vaccine Candidate Against COVID-19 Achieved Success in First Interim Analysis from Phase 3 Study," Pfizer press release, November 9, 2020.

15 Morgan Phillips, "Trump says Pfizer's Operation Warp Speed participation denial is an 'unfortunate misrepresentation,'" Fox Business, November 13, 2020.

16 Mary Papenfuss, "Pfizer Declines Invitation To White House 'Vaccine Summit,'" HuffPost, December 7, 2020—quote from that article: "A spokesperson for Moderna, which is also awaiting Food and Drug Administration approval for the use of its COVID-19 vaccine, said in a statement that Operation Warp Speed contacted the company 'to be part of a meeting at the White House concerning COVID-19 vaccine plans' and that Moderna 'indicated its willingness to participate,' Stat reported. The company learned later that 'based on the meeting's agenda, its participation would not be required,' the statement noted. An FDA representative insisted on Monday that the drugmakers had actually been excluded from the meeting because agency officials were concerned about the impropriety of executives mingling at the White House with FDA members who are charged with approving their vaccines, Bloomberg reported."
Shanthie Rexaline, "Pfizer, Moderna Opt Out Of White House Vaccine Summit: Report," Yahoo Finance, December 8, 2020.
Lev Facher, "Pfizer and Moderna decline invitations to White House 'Vaccine Summit,'" Boston.com, December 8, 2020.

17 Stephen Collinson and Maeve Reston, "Biden defeats Trump in an election he made about character of nation and the President," CNN Politics, November 7, 2020.

18 Paul LaMonica, "Pfizer CEO Albert Bourla sold stock the day he announced promising vaccine news," CNN News, November 11, 2020.

19 Laurie McGinley, Josh Dawsey, Yasmeen Abutaleb, and Carolyn Y. Johnson, "Trump rails against 'medical deep state' after Pfizer vaccine news comes after Election Day," *Washington Post*, November 11, 2020.

20 "Pfizer CEO says he would've released vaccine data before election if possible," interview with Dan Primack, Axios, November 9, 2020.

21 "'That was easy': Kamala Harris receives Covid-19 vaccine – video," US news, *The Guardian*, December 29, 2020.

22 "Trump Poised to Lower Drug Payments to Match Foreign Prices," Bloomberg Tax, July 23, 2020.

23 "Pfizer CEO says Trump's executive orders overhauling U.S. drug pricing will upend the industry," CNBC.com, July 28, 2020.

24 "Biden's HHS Freezes Trump Insulin, Epinephrine Rule Until March," Bloomberg Law, January 21, 2021.

25 "Pfizer, unions, others donated $61.8 mln for Biden's inaugural," Reuters, April 21, 2021.

26 Pfizer Inc. profile summary, Open Secrets.org.

27 Sabrina Siddiqui and Saeed Shah, "U.S. to Donate 500 Million Covid-19 Vaccine Doses to Lower-Income Countries," *WSJ*, June 10, 2021.

28 "Port to patient: Improving country cold chains for COVID-19 vaccines," McKinsey, September 4, 2021—quote from that article: "[I]n sub-Saharan Africa…the lack of storage infrastructure at this level is the most basic challenge."

29 Lucas Manfredi, "Here's how much money Pfizer, Moderna and Johnson & Johnson could make from COVID vaccines," Fox Business, March 8, 2021.

30 Jared Hopkins, "U.S. Buys 200 Million Covid-19 Vaccines From Pfizer and BioNTech at About $24 a Shot," *WSJ*, July 23, 2021.